# a bit on the side

tempting sauces, salads and accompaniments -
over 100 essential recipes

silvana franco & nicola diggins

southwater

This edition is published by Southwater

Southwater is an imprint of Anness Publishing Ltd
Hermes House, 88–89 Blackfriars Road, London SE1 8HA
tel. 020 7401 2077; fax 020 7633 9499; info@anness.com

© Anness Publishing Ltd 1997, 2002

Published in the USA by Southwater, Anness Publishing Inc.
27 West 20th Street, New York, NY 10011; fax 212 807 6813

This edition distributed in the UK by The Manning Partnership
251–253 London Road East, Batheaston, Bath BA1 7RL
tel. 01225 852 727; fax 01225 852 852; sales@manning-partnership.co.uk

This edition distributed in the USA by National Book Network
4720 Boston Way, Lanham, MD 20706
tel. 301 459 3366; fax 301 459 1705; www.nbnbooks.com

This edition distributed in Canada by General Publishing
895 Don Mills Road, 400–402 Park Centre, Toronto, Ontario M3C 1W3
tel. 416 445 3333; fax 416 445 5991; www.genpub.com

This edition distributed in Australia by Sandstone Publishing
Unit 1, 360 Norton Street, Leichhardt, New South Wales 2040
tel. 02 9560 7888; fax 02 9560 7488; sales@sandstonepublishing.com.au

This edition distributed in New Zealand by The Five Mile Press (NZ) Ltd
PO Box 33-1071 Takapuna, Unit 11/101-111 Diana Drive, Glenfield, Auckland 10
tel. (09) 444 4144; fax (09) 444 4518; fivemilenz@clear.net.nz

A CIP catalogue record for this book is available from the British Library.

*Publisher:* Joanna Lorenz
*Managing Editor:* Linda Fraser
*Assistant Editor:* Margaret Malone
*Designers:* Kim Bale, Visual Image and Brian Weldon
*Photographers:* William Adams-Lingwood, Edward Allwright and James Duncan
*Home Economists:* Lucy McKelvie, Jenny Shapter and Elizabeth Silver
*Additional Recipes:* Maxine Clark, Jenny Stacey and Steven Wheeler

Previously published as *Over the Top … and on the Side*

1 3 5 7 9 10 8 6 4 2

## NOTES

For all recipes, quantities are given in both metric and imperial measures and, where appropriate, measures are also
given in standard cups and spoons. Follow one set, but not a mixture, because they are not interchangeable.

Standard spoon and cup measures are level. 1 tsp = 5ml, 1 tbsp = 15ml, 1 cup = 250ml/8fl oz

Australian standard tablespoons are 20ml. Australian readers should use 3 tsp in place of 1 tbsp for measuring small
quantities of gelatine, cornflour, salt, etc.

Medium eggs are used unless otherwise stated.

# a bit on the

side

# Contents

# INTRODUCTION

Light or creamy, rich or tangy, fiery or mild, a sauce, salsa, relish or marinade will transform any dish from the entirely ordinary to the simply divine. Choosing the correct sauce is all important – it should enhance the dish it is served with and not overpower it. The simple classic sauces are easy to select since they are traditionally served with foods that they go particularly well with: mint sauce with lamb, apple sauce with pork, or cranberry with turkey, for instance. The more complicated classic sauces can generally be served with a broader range of dishes and you'll find that the recipes in this section often have several serving suggestions. The three chapters that follow provide a selection of traditional and contemporary sauces for meat, poultry, fish, seafood, pasta and vegetables.

A sauce isn't always added after cooking – it may also be an essential part of a dish, like those in the marinade chapter. In these the flavours blend so well, that you are hardly aware of the sauce at all.

Salsas, which are fresh, uncooked sauces, have become very fashionable. Simple to prepare and very versatile, these flavourful mixtures can be served either as a dip or as a sauce. They can be fruity, fiery or creamy and are delicious with all sorts of foods from tortilla chips and crudités to grilled chicken and fish.

The final two savoury chapters include a wide range of tart and tangy relishes, cool creamy yogurt raitas, delicious dips and a selection of dressings for salads.

Sauces, of course, aren't always savoury; the final chapter provides a delectable selection of sweet sauces to serve with desserts. There are creamy sauces and custards to serve with fruit pies and crumbles, tart fruit sauces, a rich fudgy chocolate sauce and fresh and fruity salsas to serve with ice creams.

The introduction is packed with information on ingredients and there are professional cook's tips on sauce-making techniques. So, whether you are an experienced cook, or never previously ventured further than the ketchup bottle, *over the top... and on the side* will provide inspiration to liven up your meals.

# Fruit

The varying colours, flavours and textures of fruit make them the ideal ingredient for many salsas, relishes and dips.

**Bananas**
Packed with nutrients and full of flavour, it's worth being sure that the bananas you buy are at their best. Choose fruit that are deep yellow, firm to the touch and without black spots on them.

**Melons**
There are lots of different melons available depending upon the time of year. Crisp-fleshed watermelons and juicy, orange-fleshed melons, such as Charentais, make super fruity salsas.

**Papayas**
Also known as paw paw, the papaya is a sweet-fleshed fruit with edible seeds. It is rich in vitamin A and acts as a very good digestive when served at the end of a meal.

**Pineapples**
Pineapple can be used in both sweet and savoury dishes but must be served when ripe and fresh. Choose fruit that feels firm, with a definite pineapple aroma; a leaf pulled from the centre should come away easily.

**Passion fruit**
Cut the fruit in half to reveal the succulent, aromatic pulp and edible seeds. Serve with other tropical fruit or with ice cream.

**Mangoes**
Mango is wonderful for serving fresh in salsas and dips or cooking down into sweet chutney. The ripeness of mango is not determined by colour: to test the fruit, press it gently and the flesh should give slightly when ripe.

**Oranges**
The juice, flesh and grated rind of oranges are both fragrant and flavoursome. Use them to add a delicious tangy sparkle to sauces, relishes and fruity salsas.

# Vegetables

From juicy sweet-fleshed tomatoes to the smooth and creamy-textured avocado – vegetables make an ideal base for, or a colourful crunchy addition to, all sorts of salsas, relishes and dips.

### Avocados

The skin and large stone of the avocado are inedible. The flesh, however, can be mashed until smooth and creamy to make a perfect salsa base. Avocado discolours quickly, so brush cut surfaces with lemon juice to preserve them, and use any avocado-based salsa soon after mixing.

### Cucumbers

Cool refreshing cucumbers chosen for salsas and crudités must feel firm to the touch. The skin adds texture and fibre, so avoid peeling them.

### Onions

Spring onions, red onions, shallots and everyday onions are all frequently used in salsas, relishes and dips. Spring onions and red onions are mild enough to serve raw, while shallots and ordinary onions melt into sweetness when cooked gently over a low heat.

### Peppers

Red, yellow and orange peppers have a sweet flavour that is enhanced by roasting and grilling. Green peppers taste fresh and herby and are best sliced, served raw in salads or salsas.

### Sweetcorn

If buying fresh corn cobs, choose plump cobs with tightly packed kernels. Remove the papery leaves and silks or husk and boil in plain water (salt toughens the kernels) for 5 minutes, until bright yellow. Lift out of the water, season with salt and smother with butter.

### Tomatoes

The most essential salsa ingredient – opt for plump, firm-fleshed tomatoes that are a good shade of red. Though available all year, tomatoes are at their best in summer, simply because they are often grown in hot-houses during winter months and are then not only expensive but also lacking in flavour.

# Spices and Flavourings

Whereas herbs are generally the leaf parts of a plant, spices may be made from the seeds, bark, stems or roots. They are usually dried and may be sold whole or ground. As with herbs, keep them in airtight jars in a dark cupboard, particularly ground spices which loose their flavour more quickly than their whole counterparts. For the fullest flavour buy in small quantities and use up quickly.

**Capers**
These give a piquant note and are particularly good with fish.

**Cardamoms**
These oval, light green pods are very aromatic. They can be used whole or the seeds removed and crushed for a warm spicy flavour.

**Chillies and Cayenne**
Fresh and dried chillies add heat and vary according to size and colour. Generally, but not always, large, pale green chillies will be milder than small red ones. Dried chillies are always hotter than fresh. Cayenne is a very hot chilli. Wash your hands thoroughly after preparing chillies and if possible wear thin rubber gloves.

**Cinnamon sticks**
This is the sweetly flavoured rolled bark of a tropical evergreen tree. It can be bought ground, but the sticks give a mellow flavour to syrups and are easily removed.

**Cloves**
The plump, dried flower buds from an evergreen tree. They are aromatic with a faint bitter taste.

**Coriander seeds**
A sweet, warm aromatic spice, also available ground.

**Garlic**
A strongly flavoured member of the onion family, and should therefore be used in moderation. For less a pungent flavour, increase the cooking time. The pinky-purple cloves are considered to have a better flavour than the white varieties.

**Ginger, fresh and dried**
Fresh root ginger is the plump bulbous rhizome of the ginger plant. It is knobbly and should be peeled thinly with a potato peeler or sharp knife and chopped or grated. It has a hot, sharp, fresh taste quite different from ground ginger which is hot and peppery.

**Juniper berries**
These small purply-black berries have a sweet resinous aroma which can be released by crushing with a heavy-bladed knife before use.

**Lemon grass**
The bulbous base of this lemon-scented grass is usually used. It can be crushed and used whole or chopped for a stronger flavour.

**Mace**
This is the thin lacy cover of the nutmeg seed and has a similar, though more gentle, flavour. It is sold ground although whole mace is sometimes available.

**Mustard**
Comes as brown, black or white seed as well as traditional mustard powder, ground mustard seed blended with turmeric. It is a great flavour enhancer for cheese and egg sauces but should be used in moderation as it can be hot.

**Nutmeg**
Is the ripened dried seed of a large tropical tree. It has a rich mellow flavour which is greatly enhanced if freshly grated.

**Paprika**
A sweet, piquant spice, ideal for enhancing the flavour of vegetables and meat.

**Peppercorns**
Pepper is a universal seasoning. Dried black and white peppercorns are best freshly ground for the most pungency. Green peppercorns are available fresh, bottled in brine or dried.

**Saffron**
This is the dried thread-like stigma of a crocus. It gives a rich golden yellow colour and slightly musty sweet flavour to sauces.

**Shallots**
These are another member of the onion family and have a strong but more mellow flavour than the ordinary onion.

**Turmeric**
Like saffron, turmeric also gives a rich yellow colour to any sauce. Use in moderation as too much will leave an acrid bitter taste.

**Vanilla pod**
Used whole for a rich flavour.

*nutmeg*

*green cardamoms*

*cayenne*

*juniper berries*

*mace*

*saffron*

*dried ginger*

*chilli*

*fresh root ginger*

*turmeric*

*coriander seeds*

*shallots*

*cloves*

*capers*

*green chilli*

*red chillies*

*mustard*

*lemon grass*

*black peppercorns*

*paprika*

*cinnamon sticks*

*green peppercorns*

*vanilla pod*

*garlic*

# Herbs

Herbs are simply edible plants whose leaves have a particularly strong flavour or aroma when they are crushed or heated. It is usual to use just the leaves stripped from coarse stalks, but occasionally softer stalks and flowers are used too.

By far the best way to use herbs is straight from the garden. You'll find they can be grown in a comparatively small area and given a sunny position most will thrive on poor soils or, failing that, pot a few up and stand on a brightly lit window-sill. Supermarkets now offer an increasing selection of pot-grown or prepacked fresh herbs. These are fine, especially out of season when there is little available from the garden; however, they can be soft and do not have the robust flavour of a freshly-picked garden crop.

Dried herbs are also useful in winter but a number lose their flavour and acquire hay-like overtones during drying and storage. Choose freeze-dried brands for the best flavour and store in airtight containers in a dark cupboard. Glass jars on a brightly lit spice rack may look attractive but are not ideal for the purpose.

**Bay**
Has dark green, leathery leaves which are generally used whole to impart a delicate flavour to sauces. To increase the flavour crush the leaf in your hand or tear into pieces. It is an essential component of a bouquet garni.

**Chervil**
A very delicate herb with soft, lacy, fern-like leaves. It has a very mild aniseed flavour so use plenty of it and only add near the end of cooking.

**Chives**
These have slender, cylindrical, grass-like leaves with a mild onion flavour. Use fresh with egg and cheese dishes.

**Coriander**
Coriander, with its finely scalloped broad leaf, has a spicy flavour. Leaves and stalks can be used, particularly fresh in salsas. It is essential in Indian dishes.

**Dill**
A distinctive, pungent herb with blue-green feathery leaves. It goes well with fish and egg dishes and also cream sauces.

**Mint**
Well known for its freshly flavoured, bright green leaves. Traditionally used with lamb, it is also good with fish and some vegetable dishes.

**Oregano and marjoram**
These herbs are from the same family. They both have small, oval, peppery-flavoured leaves which enhance tomato-based sauces. Oregano has a more robust flavour than sweeter marjoram.

**Parsley**
Two varieties of this widely-used herb are available, curly parsley and flat-leaf parsley. Flat-leaf parsley has a more concentrated flavour but curly parsley is more easily chopped. If using parsley in a marinade, stock or bouquet garni, use most of the stalk as this has a more concentrated flavour.

**Rosemary**
Rosemary has aromatic needle-like leaves. They are coarse and pungent so use sparingly and chop very finely.

**Tarragon**
With its long, narrow, glossy leaves and warm, aniseed flavour tarragon is an essential sauce flavouring. Use fresh French tarragon rather than Russian or dried tarragon.

**Thyme**
This herb has tiny oval leaves with a strong flavour and goes well with most dishes. Some varieties have a lemon scent which goes well with chicken and fish dishes. It is coarse, so remove the leaves from the stalks.

*flat-leaf parsley*

*tarragon*

*parsley*

chives

dill

chervil

mint

coriander

thyme

rosemary

oregano

bay

marjoram

# Instant Dips

Whip up some speedy dips for an impromptu cocktail party or to impress unexpected guests with the help of storecupboard classics, such as mayonnaise, sun-dried tomatoes and soy sauce.

## Creamy black olive dip

To make a great dip for bread sticks, stir a little black olive paste into a carton of extra thick double cream until smooth and well blended. Add salt and freshly ground black pepper and a squeeze of fresh lemon juice to taste. Serve chilled. For a low-calorie version, substitute low-fat or Greek-style natural yogurt for the cream.

## Crème fraîche or soured cream with spring onions

Finely chop a bunch of spring onions and stir into a carton of crème fraîche or soured cream. Add a dash of chilli sauce, a squeeze of fresh lime juice and a little salt and freshly ground black pepper to taste. Serve with tortilla chips or alongside a spicy guacamole.

## Greek-style yogurt and grainy mustard dip

Mix a small carton of creamy Greek-style yogurt with one or two teaspoons of wholegrain mustard. Serve with grissini or crudités.

## Herby mayonnaise

Liven up ready-made French-style mayonnaise with a handful of chopped fresh herbs – try flat-leaf parsley, basil, dill or tarragon. Season to taste with plenty of freshly ground black pepper and serve with crisp carrot and cucumber batons.

## Passata and horseradish dip

Bring a little tang to a small carton or bottle of passata (sieved tomatoes) by adding some horseradish sauce or a teaspoon or two of creamed horseradish. Add salt and pepper to taste and serve with spicy tortilla chips.

## Pesto dip

For a simple, speedy Italian-style dip, stir a tablespoon of ready-made red or green pesto into a carton of soured cream. Serve with crisp crudités or wedges of oven-roasted Mediterranean vegetables, such as peppers, courgettes and onions.

## Soft cheese and chive dip

Mix a tub of skimmed milk soft cheese with two or three tablespoons of snipped fresh chives and season to taste with salt and plenty of black pepper. If the dip is a little too thick, stir in a spoonful or two of milk to soften it.

## Spiced yogurt dip

To make a speedy Indian-style dip, stir a little mild or hot and spicy curry paste into a carton of natural yogurt. Add a finely chopped apple or a spoonful or two of mango chutney and serve with crisp poppadoms.

## Yogurt and sun-dried tomato dip

Stir one or two tablespoons of sun-dried tomato paste into a carton of Greek-style yogurt. Season to taste with salt and freshly ground black pepper. Serve with small triangles of crisp toasted pitta bread or salted crisps. Alternatively use soured cream in place of the yogurt.

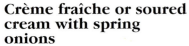

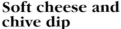

*Creamy black
olive dip*

*Crème fraîche with
spring onions*

*Yogurt and
sun-dried tomato dip*

*Herby
mayonnaise*

*Greek-style
yogurt and grainy
mustard dip*

*Soft cheese
and chive
dip*

*Spiced yogurt dip*

*Pesto dip*

*Passata and
horseradish dip*

# Serving Suggestions

There are many ways to serve salsas, relishes and dips: they can be spooned on to the side, or over the top, of fish, chicken or meat dishes, used as a sandwich filling or topping, or served with anti-pasti or cheese. One of the fun ways to serve them is with a selection of titbits for dipping.

### Bread sticks
Choose crunchy Italian-style grissini bread sticks for thick and creamy dips and salsas. To serve them, either pile the bread sticks on to a plate or in a large bowl, or stand them in a tall glass or jug.

### Cheese straws
These are ideal for dipping and dunking. You can buy cheese straws ready-made, but they are very easy to make at home. Simply roll out a small packet of puff pastry thinly and cut it into strips. Lightly brush the strips with beaten egg and sprinkle with a little grated cheese. (Twist the strips first, if you like.) Chill for 10 minutes, then bake them at 180°C/ 350°F/Gas 4 for 15–20 minutes or until puffed and golden. Cool on a wire rack before serving.

### Corn chips
These crisp ready-made Mexican-style snacks are now widely available in delicatessens and supermarkets. Choose cheese-flavoured corn chips for creamy dips and the plain variety for spicier tomato-based salsas. Look out for tasty blue corn chips in speciality shops and food halls.

### Fruit crudités
These make the perfect accompaniment to sweet dips. Cut chunks of peach, nectarine, pear, banana or apple and arrange on a platter with whole strawberries, segments of oranges, plums, sharon fruit or not-too-ripe figs.

### Potato crisps
Salted crisps, either the plain variety or one of the many flavours, are a popular storecupboard standby and make a great accompaniment to absolutely any dip. Choose the thicker ones for chunky or very thick dips and only serve light, creamy dips with the more fragile varieties.

### Tortilla chips
The classic accompaniment to chilled tomato salsa, tortilla chips are now available in a variety of flavours. Serve the fiery chips with creamy dips and the cool ones with robust salsas or relishes.

### Vegetable crisps
There are some brands of vegetable crisps available to buy ready-made, but they are also easy to make at home. Several different vegetables work well, try sweet potato, beetroot, carrot, parsnip or, of course, potato. Peel the vegetables, slice them wafer-thin with a mandoline or swivel-style vegetable peeler, then deep fry the slices in hot vegetable oil and season them with plenty of salt and a little chilli powder, paprika or cayenne pepper.

### Vegetable crudités
Chunks, sticks or wedges of fresh raw vegetables make brilliant scoops for all manner of dips and salsas. Try sticks of carrot, celery and cucumber; cut thin strips of more than one colour of pepper; or trim small florets of cauliflower or broccoli. To make wedges or "scoops", cut small peppers lengthways into thin wedges, trim celery into short lengths, or cut 5 cm/2 in pieces of cucumber into six lengthways and remove the seeds. Crisp chicory leaves and the small central leaves from cos or Little Gem lettuces also make delicious crudités.

Cheese straws and
bread sticks

Fruit
crudités

Vegetable
crudités

Corn chips

Tortilla chips

Vegetable crisps

Potato crisps

## Stocks

Many sauces depend for their depth and richness on a good quality stock base. Fresh stock will give the most balanced flavor and it is worth the effort to make it at home. It may be frozen successfully for several months. Canned beef bouillon and chicken broth are good substitutes. For everyday cooking, most cooks will use stock cubes, but these often have a salt base so taste carefully and season lightly.

### FISH STOCK

INGREDIENTS
any fish bones, skin and
   trimmings available
1 onion
1 carrot
1 celery stalk
6 black peppercorns
2 bay leaves
3 stalks parsley

**1** Peel and coarsely slice the onion. Peel and chop the carrot, and scrub and slice the celery.

**2** Place all the ingredients in a large saucepan and add enough water to cover. Bring to a boil, skim the surface and simmer uncovered for 20 minutes.

**3** Strain and use immediately or store for two days in the refrigerator.

### BROWN STOCK

INGREDIENTS
2 tbsp vegetable oil
3 lb shin, shank or neck of beef
   bones, cut into pieces
8 oz shin of beef, cut into pieces
bouquet garni
2 onions, trimmed and quartered
2 carrots, scrubbed and chopped
2 celery sticks, sliced
1 tsp black peppercorns
1/2 tsp salt

**1** Drizzle the vegetable oil over the bottom of a roasting pan, add the bones and meat. Coat in oil and bake at 425°F for 25–30 minutes or until well browned, turning regularly during cooking.

**2** Transfer the meat and bones to a large saucepan, add the remaining ingredients and cover with 14 cups of water. Bring to the boil, skim the surface, then partially cover and simmer for 2¹/₂–3 hours or until reduced to 7 cups.

**3** Strain the stock into a bowl. Cool and remove the solidified fat before use. Store for up to 4 days in the refrigerator.

# CHICKEN OR WHITE STOCK

INGREDIENTS
1 onion
4 cloves
1 carrot
2 leeks
2 celery sticks
1 chicken carcass, cooked or raw,
    or 750 g/1½ lb veal bones cut
    into pieces
bouquet garni
8 black peppercorns
2.5 ml/½ tsp salt

**1** Peel the onion, cut into quarters and spike each quarter with a clove. Scrub and roughly chop the vegetables.

**2** Break up the chicken carcass and place in a large saucepan with the remaining ingredients.

**3** Cover with 1.7 litres/3 pints/7 cups water. Bring to the boil, skim the surface and simmer, partially covered for 2 hours. Strain the stock into a bowl and allow to cool. When cold remove the hardened fat before using. Store for up to 4 days in the refrigerator.

# VEGETABLE STOCK

INGREDIENTS
30 ml/2 tbsp vegetable oil
1 onion
2 carrots
2 large celery sticks, plus any
    small amounts from the
    following: leeks, celeriac,
    parsnip, turnip, cabbage or
    cauliflower trimmings,
    mushrooms peelings
bouquet garni
6 black peppercorns

**1** Peel, halve and slice the onion. Roughly chop the remaining vegetables.

**2** Heat the oil in a large pan and fry the onion and vegetables until soft and lightly browned. Add the remaining ingredients and cover with 1.7 litres/3 pints/7 cups water.

**3** Bring to the boil, skim the surface then partially cover and simmer for 1½ hours. Strain the stock and allow to cool. Store in the refrigerator for 2–3 days.

# Thickening a Sauce

The simplest way to turn a liquid into a richer, more delicious sauce is to reduce it by bringing to a rolling boil over a high heat. However, there are many other methods, depending on the ingredients used in the dish you are cooking.

## ROUX BASES

A roux, flour cooked gently in butter or oil, is the most common method of thickening. Generally equal quantities of butter and flour are used and the length of cooking time determines the type of sauce produced.

*Roux blanc*

*Roux blond*

*Roux brun*

## ROUX BLANC

Melt the butter slowly then quickly stir in the flour. Continue cooking over a low heat for 1-2 minutes before removing from the heat and gradually adding hot liquid. This method will produce a white sauce.

## ROUX BLOND

Made in the same way but the flour and butter are cooked for 3-4 minutes until they turn a pale straw colour.

## ROUX BRUN

Again the butter and flour are cooked, but this time for 7-8 minutes until a pale nut brown colour. Stir continuously as it will easily burn.

# BEURRE MANIÉ

If you have an unknown quantity of liquid to thicken, perhaps the liquid left over from a casserole or pot roast, then this method is ideal. Equal quantities of flour and butter are blended together, then small pea-sized pieces are stirred into the hot liquid, brought back to the boil and stirred until thickened.

*Beurre manié*

# CORNFLOUR

A fine chalky flour ground from maize, 15 ml/1 tbsp will thicken 300 ml/½ pint of liquid. Blend the cornflour to a paste with 30 ml/2 tbsp of cold water then stir into the hot liquid and cook for 1-2 minutes until thickened.

*cornflour*

# ARROWROOT

A powdery starch derived from the roots of the maranta plant. Used in a similar way to cornflour it will give a clearer sauce. Remove from the heat as soon as it thickens as it can be unstable.

*arrowroot*

# EGG YOLKS AND CREAM

Blended egg yolks and cream make a rich sauce. Two egg yolks blended with 45-60 ml/3-4 tbsp of cream will thicken 300 ml/½ pint of liquid. Stir a little hot sauce into the egg and cream mixture then return to the rest of the liquid. Stir over a gentle heat until the sauce coats the back of a spoon. For extra care, cook in a double boiler or in a bowl over a saucepan of hot water.

*egg yolks and cream*

# Preparing Tomatoes

Flame-skinning tomatoes is the simplest and quickest method.

**1** Skewer one tomato at a time on a metal fork and hold in a gas flame for 1–2 minutes, turning it until the skin splits and wrinkles.

**2** Leave the tomatoes until cool enough to handle, then slip off and discard the skins.

**3** Halve the tomatoes, then scoop out the seeds using a teaspoon.

**4** Finely chop the tomatoes using a small sharp knife and use as required.

## COOK'S TIP
If you don't have a gas cooker, simply place the tomatoes in a bowl of boiling water for 30–60 seconds, until the skin splits. Rinse the tomatoes under cold water, then peel.

# Preparing Cucumber

Cucumber can be cut into strips and then softened for use in delicate salsas by salting.

**1** Trim off the ends from the cucumber and cut it into 2.5 cm/1 in lengths, then slice each piece lengthways into thin strips.

**2** Place the cucumber slices in a colander and sprinkle with 5 ml/1 tsp salt. Leave for 5 minutes until wilted.

**3** Wash the cucumber slices well under cold running water, then drain and pat them dry with kitchen paper.

# Preparing Chillies

The hottest chillies need very careful handling – just follow these simple steps. If you do touch chillies, wash your hands thoroughly.

# Peeling Peppers

Peppers are delicious added raw to salads. However, roasting them first softens the flesh and gives them a delicious warm flavour.

**1** To remove the skin from habanero chillies, skewer the chillies, one at a time, on a metal fork and hold over a gas flame for 2–3 minutes, turning the chilli until the skin blackens and blisters.

**2** Leave the chillies to cool for a few minutes, then use a clean dish towel to rub off the skins.

**1** Preheat the grill to medium. Place the peppers on a baking sheet and grill for 8–12 minutes, turning regularly, until the skins have blackened and blistered.

**2** Place the peppers in a bowl and cover with a clean dish towel. Leave for 5 minutes so the steam helps to lift the skin away from the flesh.

**3** Try not to touch the chillies with your bare hands; use a fork to hold them and slice them open with a sharp knife.

**4** Even the less hot varieties of chillies can be fairly fiery. To reduce the heat, cut the chillies in half and scrape out the seeds using the tip of a knife.

**3** When the peppers are cool enough to handle, pierce a hole in the bottom of each one and gently squeeze out the juices into a bowl.

**4** Peel off and discard the skins from the peppers and then chop or slice as required in recipes.

# Keeping Sauces Warm

There is nothing more unappetizing than a congealed sauce, so keeping sauces warm successfully is essential. It can sometimes be tricky: the more delicate cream- and butter-based sauces curdle easily, whilst flour-based sauces may thin with prolonged heating. Follow the advice below to prevent a skin forming whilst keeping the sauce at a reasonable temperature.

**1** Pour the sauce into a double boiler or a bowl suspended over a pan of hot, not boiling, water. To prevent a skin forming on a cream and butter sauce, cover the surface of the sauce with buttered greaseproof paper or clearfilm.

## COOK'S TIP

All these types of sauces can also be kept warm in a vacuum flask. Make sure the flask is reasonably new and free of any stains or lingering smells. You may find that keeping the sauce in a flask alters its flavour, so this method should only be used as a last resort. Remember to heat the flask first with boiling water before gently pouring in the warm sauce.

**2** For flour-based sauces, spoon over a little melted butter.

**3** For sweet sauces, sprinkle the surface with caster sugar.

## Bread Sauce

Smooth and surprisingly delicate, this old-fashioned sauce is traditionally served with roast chicken, turkey and game birds. If you'd prefer a less strong flavor, reduce the number of cloves and add a little freshly grated nutmeg instead.

### Serves 6

INGREDIENTS
4 cloves
1 small onion
bay leaf
1¼ cup milk
2 cups fresh white breadcrumbs
1 tbsp butter
1 tbsp light cream
salt and pepper

*breadcrumbs*

*milk*

*cloves*

*cream*

*onion*

*butter*

*bay leaf*

**1** Peel the onion and stick the cloves into it. Put it into a saucepan with the bay leaf and pour in the milk.

**2** Bring to a boil then remove from the heat and steep for 15–20 minutes. Remove the bay leaf and onion.

**3** Return to the heat and stir in the crumbs. Simmer for 4–5 minutes or until thick and creamy.

**4** Stir in the butter and cream, then season to taste.

# Horseradish Sauce

This light, creamy sauce has a piquant, peppery flavor that's spiced with just a hint of mustard. It is the classic accompaniment to roast beef, but is perfect, too, with herby sausages and grilled fish.

*Serves 6*

INGREDIENTS
3 in piece fresh horseradish
1 tbsp lemon juice
2 tsp sugar
$\frac{1}{2}$ tsp English mustard powder
$\frac{2}{3}$ cup heavy cream

*cream*

*horseradish*

*mustard*

*caster sugar*

*lemon*

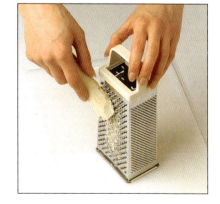

**1** Scrub and peel the horseradish.

**2** Grate the horseradish as finely as you can.

**3** Mix together the horseradish, lemon juice, sugar and mustard powder.

**4** Whip the cream until it stands in soft peaks then gently fold in the horseradish mixture.

# Apple Sauce

Really more of a condiment than a sauce, this tart puree is usually served cold or warm, rather than hot. It's typically served with rice, roast pork or duck, but is also good with cold meats and savory pies.

*Serves 6*

INGREDIENTS
8 oz tart cooking apples
2 tbsp water
thin strip lemon rind
1 tbsp butter
1–2 tbsp sugar

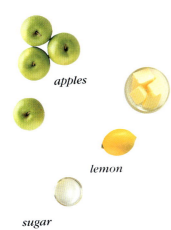

*apples*

*water*

*lemon*

*sugar*

**1** Peel, core and slice the apples.

**2** Place the apples in a saucepan with the water and lemon peel. Cook uncovered over a low heat until very soft, stirring occasionally.

**3** Remove the lemon rind, then beat to a pulp with a spoon or press through a strainer.

**4** Stir in the butter and then add sugar to taste.

# Cranberry Sauce

This is the sauce for roast turkey, but don't just keep it for festive occasions. The vibrant color and tart taste are a perfect partner to any white roast meat, and it makes a great addition to a chicken sandwich.

*Serves 6*

INGREDIENTS
1 orange
8 oz cranberries
1¼ cups sugar

*orange*

*granulated sugar*

*cranberries*

**1** Pare the rind thinly from the orange, taking care not to remove any white pith. Squeeze the juice.

**2** Place in a saucepan with the cranberries, sugar and ²/₃ cup water.

**3** Bring to a boil, stirring until the sugar has dissolved, then simmer for 10–15 minutes or until the berries burst.

**4** Remove the rind and allow to cool before serving.

# Mint Sauce

Tart, yet sweet, this simple sauce is the perfect foil to rich meat. It's best served, of course, with new season's roast lamb, but is wonderful, too, with grilled lamb chops or pan-fried duck.

*Serves 6*

INGREDIENTS
small bunch mint
1 tbsp sugar
2 tbsp boiling water
3 tbsp white wine vinegar

*white wine vinegar*

*mint*

*sugar*

**I** Strip the leaves from the stalks.

**2** Chop the leaves very finely.

**3** Place in a bowl with the sugar and pour on the boiling water. Stir well and let stand for 5–10 minutes.

**4** Add the vinegar and let stand for 1–2 hours before serving.

# Tangy Orange Sauce
## *SAUCE BIGARADE*

A tangy orange sauce for roast duck and rich game. For a full mellow flavour it is best made with the rich roasting-pan juices, but butter makes an admirable substitute if these aren't available.

*Serves 4-6*

INGREDIENTS
roasting pan juices or 25 g/1 oz/ 2 tbsp butter
40 g/1½ oz/3 tbsp plain flour
300 ml/½ pint/1¼ cups hot stock (preferably duck)
150 ml/¼ pint/ cup red wine
2 Seville oranges or 2 sweet oranges plus 2 tsp lemon juice
15 ml/1 tbsp orange-flavoured liqueur
30 ml/2 tbsp redcurrant jelly
salt and pepper

red wine

roasting-pan juices

plain flour

orange-flavoured liqueur

butter

redcurrant jelly

lemon     oranges

**1** Pour off any excess fat from the roasting pan leaving the juices, or melt the butter in a small pan.

**2** Sprinkle in the flour and cook, stirring continuously for 4 minutes or until lightly browned.

**3** Off the heat, gradually blend in the hot stock and wine. Bring to the boil, stirring continuously. Lower the heat and simmer gently for 5 minutes.

**4** Meanwhile, using a citrus zester, peel the rind thinly from one orange. Squeeze the juice from both oranges.

**5** Blanch the rind; place it in a small pan, cover with water and bring to the boil. Cook for 5 minutes, drain and add the rind to the sauce.

**6** Add the orange juice, liqueur and jelly to the sauce, stirring until the jelly has dissolved. Season to taste and pour over the jointed duckling or game.

# Spicy Redcurrant Sauce

## *CUMBERLAND SAUCE*

Spicy yet sweet, this redcurrant sauce is tailor-made for gammon and ham. A string of translucent, jewel-like redcurrants would make an excellent summery garnish for a dish served with this sauce.

*Serves 8*

INGREDIENTS
1 lemon
1 orange
2 sugar lumps
150 ml/$\frac{1}{4}$ pint port
4 allspice berries
4 cloves
5 ml/1 tsp mustard seeds
225 g/8 oz redcurrant jelly
10 ml/2 tsp arrowroot
30 ml/2 tbsp orange liqueur
pinch of ground ginger

*port*

*redcurrant jelly*        *arrowroot*

*sugar lumps, cloves and allspice berries*

*lemon*

*orange liqueur*

*orange*        *ground ginger*

**1** Peel the lemon thinly so that no white pith is removed. Cut into thin strips with a sharp knife or scissors, or peel the lemon with a citrus zester.

**2** Blanch the rind; place in a small pan. Cover with water, bring to the boil, cook for 5 minutes, drain and reserve the rinds.

**3** Wash the orange, then rub it all over with the sugar lumps until they are saturated with oil.

**4** In a small pan bring the port, sugar lumps and whole spices to the boil. Remove from the heat and cool. Strain the port into a pan, add the jelly and stir over a low heat until dissolved.

## COOK'S TIP
To develop a rich spicy flavour, store this sauce in the fridge for 2–3 days then bring to room temperature before serving.

**5** Blend the arrowroot with the orange liqueur and stir into the sauce. Bring to the boil and cook for 1–2 minutes until it has thickened.

**6** Remove from the heat and add the rinds and ground ginger to taste. Cool to room temperature before serving with hot or cold gammon slices or grilled lamb cutlets.

# Mushroom and Wine Sauce

## *SAUCE CHASSEUR*

This excellent sauce will transform simple pan-fried or grilled chicken and light meats into a dinner-party dish.

*Serves 3–4*

INGREDIENTS
25 g/1 oz/2 tbsp butter
1 shallot, finely chopped
115 g/4 oz button mushrooms, sliced
120 ml/4 fl oz/$\frac{1}{2}$ cup white wine
30 ml/2 tbsp brandy
1 quantity Sauce Espagnole
15 ml/1 tbsp chopped fresh tarragon or chervil

*brandy*

*white wine*

*butter*

*shallot*

*button mushrooms*

*Sauce Espagnole*

*chervil*

## COOK'S TIP
If you don't mind the grey tinge they give to the colour, flat mushrooms have more flavour than button ones.

**1** Melt the butter and fry the shallot until soft but not brown.

**2** Add the mushrooms and sauté until they just begin to brown.

**3** Pour in the wine and brandy, and simmer over a medium heat until reduced by half.

**4** Add the Sauce Espagnole and herbs and heat through, stirring occasionally. Serve hot with grilled or roast pork, chicken or with rabbit.

# Tartare Sauce

This is an authentic tartare sauce to serve with all kinds of fish, but for a simpler version you could always stir the flavourings into mayonnaise.

## Serves 6

INGREDIENTS
2 hard-boiled eggs
1 egg yolk from a size 1 egg
10 ml/2 tsp lemon juice
175 ml/6 fl oz/³/₄ cup olive oil
5 ml/1 tsp chopped capers
5 ml/1 tsp chopped gherkin
5 ml/1 tsp chopped fresh chives
5 ml/1 tsp chopped fresh parsley
salt and pepper

chives

olive oil

hard-boiled eggs

lemon

parsley

gherkin and
capers

egg yolk

**1** Halve the hard-boiled eggs, remove the yolks and press them through a sieve into a bowl.

**2** Blend in the raw yolk and mix until smooth. Stir in the lemon juice.

**3** Add the oil very slowly, a little at a time, whisking constantly. When it begins to thicken, add the oil more quickly to form an emulsion.

**4** Finely chop one egg white and stir into the sauce with the capers, gherkins and herbs. Season to taste. Serve as an accompaniment with fried or grilled fish.

# Hollandaise Sauce

A rich butter sauce for fish and vegetables. The secret of success with this sauce is patience. Work in the butter slowly and thoroughly to give a thick, glossy texture.

*Serves 2–3*

INGREDIENTS
30 ml/2 tbsp white wine or
   tarragon vinegar
15 ml/1 tbsp water
6 black peppercorns
1 bay leaf
115 g/4 oz/½ cup butter
2 egg yolks
salt and pepper

*bay leaf*

*egg yolks*

*black peppercorns*

*butter*

*white wine vinegar*

**1** Place the vinegar, water, peppercorns, and bay leaf in a saucepan. Simmer gently until the liquid has reduced by half. Strain and cool.

**2** Cream the butter until soft.

**3** In a double saucepan or a bowl sitting over a saucepan of gently simmering, but not boiling, water, whisk together the egg yolks and vinegar until light and fluffy.

**4** Gradually add the butter a tiny piece at a time – about the size of a hazelnut will be enough. Whisk quickly until all the butter has been absorbed before adding any more.

**5** Season lightly and, if the sauce is too sharp, add a little more butter.

**6** For a thinner sauce stir in 1–2 tablespoons of single cream. Serve immediately with either steamed fish or fresh vegetables.

# Rich Brown Sauce

## SAUCE ESPAGNOLE

Espagnole is ideal for serving with red meat and game. It also makes a delicious full-flavoured base for other sauces, so make double quantity and keep some in the fridge.

### Serves 4-6

INGREDIENTS

25 g/1 oz/2 tbsp butter
50 g/2 oz bacon pieces or streaky bacon, chopped
2 shallots, chopped
1 carrot, chopped
1 celery stick, chopped
mushroom trimmings (if available)
25 g/1 oz/2 tbsp plain flour
600 ml/1 pint/2$^1$/$_2$ cups hot Brown Stock
1 bouquet garni
30 ml/2 tbsp tomato purée
15 ml/1 tbsp sherry (optional)
salt and pepper

**1** Melt the butter in a heavy-based saucepan and fry the bacon for 2–3 minutes. Add the vegetables and cook for a further 5–6 minutes until golden.

**2** Stir in the flour and cook over a medium heat for 5–10 minutes until it has become a rich brown colour.

**3** Remove from the heat and gradually blend in the stock.

*brown stock*
*carrot*
*celery*
*mushroom trimmings*
*shallots*
*sherry*
*plain flour*
*butter*
*bouquet garni*
*tomato purée*
*bacon*

**4** Slowly bring to the boil continuing to stir until the sauce thickens. Add the bouquet garni, tomato purée and seasoning. Reduce the heat and simmer gently for one hour, stirring occasionally.

**5** Strain the sauce, pressing the vegetables to extract the juice.

**6** Skim off any fat with a metal spoon. Stir in the sherry and adjust the seasoning to taste. Serve with grilled lamb chops, or other red meat.

# Creamy Madeira Sauce

## NEWBURG SAUCE

This creamy Madeira-flavoured sauce will not mask delicate foods and is therefore ideal for shellfish. It also goes well with pan-fried chicken.

*Serves 4*

INGREDIENTS
15 g/½ oz/1 tbsp butter
1 small shallot, finely chopped
cayenne pepper
300 ml/½ pint/1¼ cups double cream
60 ml/4 tbsp Madeira
salt and pepper
3 egg yolks

double cream

shallot          egg yolks

butter

cayenne
pepper      Madeira

**1** Melt the butter in a double boiler or a bowl placed over a saucepan of simmering water. Cook the shallots until they are soft.

**2** Add the cayenne and all but 60 ml/4 tbsp of the cream. Leave over the simmering water for 10 minutes to reduce slightly.

**3** Stir in the Madeira.

**4** Beat the yolks with the remaining cream and stir into the hot sauce. Continue stirring over barely simmering water until thickened. Season to taste. Spoon over seafood or chicken, reserving some for pouring, and serve immediately. Garnish with fresh herbs.

## COOK'S TIP
For a luxurious festive look, stir in 15–30 ml/1–2 tbsp of pink or black lumpfish roe.

# White Sauce

This basic recipe is wonderfully adaptable, but can be bland so always taste and season carefully.

## Serves 6

INGREDIENTS
600 ml/1 pint/2¹/₂ cups milk
25 g/1 oz/2 tbsp plain flour
25 g/1 oz/2 tbsp butter
salt and pepper

*plain flour*          *milk*

*butter*

*salt and pepper*

**1** Warm the milk in a saucepan over a low heat, but do not boil.

**2** In a separate saucepan melt the butter, then stir in the flour and cook gently for 1–2 minutes. Do not allow the roux to brown.

**3** Off the heat, gradually blend in the milk, stirring vigorously after each addition to prevent lumps forming. Bring to the boil slowly and continue to stir all the time until the sauce thickens. Simmer gently for a further 3–4 minutes to thicken. Season to taste.

## VARIATIONS

PARSLEY SAUCE is traditionally served with bacon, fish and broad beans. Stir in 15 ml/2 tbsp finely chopped fresh parsley.

CHEESE SAUCE may be used for egg and vegetable gratins. Stir in 50 g/2 oz/¹/₂ cup finely grated mature Cheddar and 2.5 ml/¹/₂ tsp prepared mustard.

## COOK'S TIP

For a thicker, coating sauce, increase the amount of flour to 50 g/2 oz/¹/₂ cup and the butter to 50 g/2 oz/4 tbsp.

# Béchamel Sauce

The creamy mellowness of the béchamel makes it ideal for lasagne as well as a base for many fish, egg and vegetable dishes.

*Serves 4*

INGREDIENTS
1 small onion
1 small carrot
1 celery stick
1 bouquet garni
6 black peppercorns
pinch freshly grated nutmeg or blade of mace
300 ml/$\frac{1}{2}$ pint/$1\frac{1}{4}$ cups milk
25 g/1 oz/2 tbsp butter
25 g/1 oz/2 tbsp plain flour
30 ml/2 tbsp single cream
salt and pepper

*bouquet garni*

*butter*

*cream*

*black peppercorns and nutmeg*

*onion*

*milk*

*plain flour*

*carrot*

*celery*

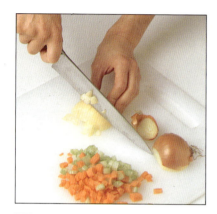

**1** Peel and finely chop the vegetables.

**2** Put the milk, vegetables and flavourings in a saucepan. Bring to the boil. Remove from the heat, cover and allow to infuse for 30 minutes.

**3** Melt the butter in a saucepan, remove from the heat and stir in the flour. Return to the heat and cook for 1–2 minutes.

**4** Reheat the flavoured milk to almost boiling. Strain into a heat-proof jug, pressing the vegetables with the back of a spoon to extract the juices.

**5** Off the heat gradually blend the milk into the roux, stirring vigorously after each addition.

**6** Bring to the boil and stir continuously until the sauce thickens. Simmer gently for 3–4 minutes. Remove from the heat, adjust the seasoning to taste and stir in the cream.

# Herby Butter Sauce

## *SAUCE BEARNAISE*

For dedicated meat-eaters, this sauce adds a note of sophistication without swamping your grilled or pan-fried steak.

*Serves 2-3*

INGREDIENTS
45 ml/3 tbsp white wine vinegar
30 ml/2 tbsp water
1 small onion, finely chopped
a few fresh tarragon and chervil sprigs
1 bay leaf
6 crushed black peppercorns
115 g/4 oz/½ cup butter
2 egg yolks
15 ml/1 tbsp chopped fresh herbs, e.g. tarragon, parsley, chervil
salt and pepper

onion

bay leaf

chervil

white wine vinegar

egg yolks

butter

parsley

tarragon

**1** Place the vinegar, water, onion, herbs and peppercorns in a saucepan. Simmer gently until the liquor is reduced by half. Strain and cool.

**2** Cream the butter until soft.

**3** In a double saucepan or a bowl over a saucepan of gently simmering water, whisk the egg yolks and liquor until light and fluffy.

**4** Gradually add the butter, half a teaspoonful at a time. Whisk until all the butter has been incorporated before adding any more.

**5** Add the chopped herbs and season to taste.

**6** Serve warm, not hot, on the side of a grilled steak or allow a good spoonful to melt over new potatoes.

# Savoury Pouring Sauce
## SAUCE VELOUTÉ

A smooth, velvety, sauce based on a white stock of fish, vegetable or meat. Choose whatever is suitable for the dish you are serving.

*Serves 4*

INGREDIENTS
600 ml/1 pint/2¹/₂ cups white stock
25 g/1 oz/2 tbsp butter
25 g/1 oz/2 tbsp plain flour
30 ml/2 tbsp single cream
salt and pepper

*butter*

*white stock*

*salt and pepper*

*single cream*

*plain flour*

**1** Warm the stock but do not boil. In another pan melt the butter and stir in the flour. Cook over a moderate heat for 3–4 minutes until a pale, straw colour, stirring continuously.

**2** Remove the pan from the heat and gradually blend in the stock. Return to the heat and bring to the boil, stirring continuously until the sauce thickens.

**3** Continue to cook at a very slow simmer, stirring occasionally, until reduced by about a quarter.

**4** Skim the surface during cooking or pour through a very fine strainer.

**5** Just before serving, remove from the heat and stir in the cream. Season to taste.

## Green Peppercorn Sauce

Green peppercorns in brine are a better choice than the dry-packed type because they give a more rounded flavour.

*Serves 3-4*

INGREDIENTS

15 ml/1 tbsp green peppercorns
  in brine, drained
1 small onion, finely chopped
25 g/1 oz/2 tbsp butter
300 ml/$\frac{1}{2}$ pint/$1\frac{1}{4}$ cups light
  stock
juice of $\frac{1}{2}$ lemon
15 ml/1 tbsp beurre manié
45 ml/3 tbsp double cream
5 ml/1 tsp Dijon mustard
salt and pepper

*lemon*

*light stock*

*green
peppercorns*

*onion*

*double cream*

*Dijon mustard*

*beurre manié*

*butter*

**1** Dry the peppercorns on absorbent kitchen paper, then crush lightly under the blade of a heavy-duty knife.

**2** Soften the onion in the butter, add the stock and lemon juice and simmer for 15 minutes.

**3** Whisk in the beurre manié a little at a time, and continue to cook until the sauce thickens.

**4** Reduce the heat and stir in the peppercorns, cream and mustard. Season to taste. Serve hot with pork steaks and buttered pasta.

# Barbecue Sauce

Brush this sauce liberally over chicken drumsticks, chops or kebabs before cooking on the barbecue, or serve as a hot or cold accompaniment to hot dogs and burgers.

*Serves 4*

INGREDIENTS
30 ml/2 tbsp vegetable oil
1 large onion, chopped
2 garlic cloves, crushed
400 g/14 oz can tomatoes
30 ml/2 tbsp Worcestershire
  sauce
15 ml/1 tbsp white wine vinegar
45 ml/3 tbsp honey
5 ml/1 tsp mustard powder
2.5 ml/$\frac{1}{2}$ tsp chilli seasoning or
  mild chilli powder
salt and pepper

*white wine vinegar*

*honey*

*onion*

*vegetable oil*

*tomatoes*

*Worcestershire sauce*

*garlic*

*mild chilli powder*

*mustard powder*

**1** Heat the oil and fry the onions and garlic until soft.

**2** Stir in the remaining ingredients and simmer, uncovered, for 15–20 minutes stirring occasionally. Cool slightly.

**3** Pour into a food processor or blender and process until smooth.

**4** Press through a sieve if you prefer and adjust the seasoning.

# Cider and Apple Cream

This sauce works excellently with grilled pork accompanied by its own garnish of rosy, glazed apple rings.

*Serves 4*

INGREDIENTS
40 g/1½ oz/3 tbsp butter
2 shallots, chopped
1 celery stick, chopped
1 carrot, chopped
25 g/1 oz/2 tbsp plain flour
450 ml/¾ pint/1⅞ cup hot, light stock
300 ml/½ pint/1¼ cups dry cider
60 ml/4 tbsp Calvados
60 ml/4 tbsp single cream
salt and pepper

FOR THE GLAZED APPLE RINGS
25 g/1 oz/2 tbsp butter
1 dessert apple, cored and sliced
1 tbsp granulated sugar

*carrot*
*plain flour*
*butter*
*light stock*   *shallots*
*granulated sugar*
*celery*
*Calvados*   *dessert apple*
*dry cider*   *single cream*

**1** Melt the butter in a pan, add the shallots, celery and carrot. Cook over a gentle heat until soft but not coloured.

**2** Sprinkle over the flour and cook over a low heat for 1–2 minutes, and make sure you stir continuously.

**3** Remove the sauce from the heat and gradually blend in the stock, cider and Calvados.

**4** Return to the heat and bring to the boil, stirring continuously until the sauce thickens. Then simmer, uncovered, until it is reduced by half.

**5** Strain into a clean pan and add the cream. Heat through and taste before seasoning as it can be salty.

## VARIATION
You could also use cider and apple cream sauce as an alternative to gravy with a traditional pork roast.

**6** For the glazed apples, melt the butter in a frying pan. Add the apple slices in a single layer and sprinkle with sugar. Cook over a moderate heat, turning occasionally until soft and lightly caramelized. Serve the sauce with pan fried or grilled pork and veal, and garnish with the glazed apples.

# Lemon and Tarragon Sauce

The sharpness of lemon and mild aniseed flavour of tarragon add zest to chicken, egg and steamed vegetable dishes.

*Serves 4*

INGREDIENTS
1 lemon
small bunch fresh tarragon
1 shallot, finely chopped
90 ml/6 tbsp white wine
1 quantity Velouté Sauce
45 ml/3 tbsp double cream
30 ml/2 tbsp brandy
salt and pepper

*shallot*

*Velouté Sauce*

*tarragon*

*lemon*

*white wine*

*brandy*

**1** Thinly pare the rind from the lemon, taking care not to remove any white pith. Squeeze the juice into a pan.

**2** Discard the coarse stalks from the tarragon. Chop the leaves and add all but 15 ml/1 tbsp to the pan with the lemon rind, shallot and wine.

**3** Simmer gently until the liquid is reduced by half. Strain into a clean pan.

**4** Add the Velouté Sauce, cream, brandy and reserved tarragon. Heat through, taste and adjust the seasoning if necessary.

COOK'S TIP
This sauce is an excellent accompaniment to pieces of boned chicken breast coverd with streaky bacon rashers and grilled or pan-fried.

# Chinese-style Sweet and Sour Sauce

A great family favourite that adds a taste of the Orient.

*Serves 4*

INGREDIENTS

1 carrot
1 green pepper
15 ml/1 tbsp vegetable oil
1 small onion, chopped
1 garlic clove, crushed
2.5 cm/1 in piece root ginger,
  peeled and grated
15 ml/$^1/_2$ tbsp cornflour
300 ml/$^1/_2$ pint/1$^1/_4$ cups
  light stock
30 ml/2 tbsp tomato purée
15 g/$^1/_2$ oz/1 tbsp soft dark
  brown sugar
30 ml/2 tbsp white wine vinegar
30 ml/2 tbsp rice wine or sherry
salt and pepper
cucumber, to garnish

*green pepper*

*light stock*

*white wine vinegar*

*onion*

*carrot*

*cornflour*

*soft dark brown sugar*

*tomato purée*

*sherry*

*garlic*

*root ginger*

**1** Peel the carrot and cut into matchstick-sized strips. Quarter the pepper, discard the stalks, seeds and membrane and cut into strips.

**2** Heat the oil and fry the onion and garlic until soft but not brown. Add the carrot, pepper and ginger and cook for a further minute. Remove from the heat.

**3** Blend the cornflour with a little stock and add to the vegetables, together with the remaining ingredients.

**4** Stir over a moderate heat until the mixture boils and thickens. Simmer uncovered for 2–3 minutes until the vegetables are just tender. Adjust the seasoning and serve with strips of stir-fried pork or chicken and with rice or noodles.

# Satay Dip

A deliciously pungent sauce which tastes great served with spicy chicken on skewers but is equally good as a dip for crisp vegetables.

*Serves 6*

INGREDIENTS

150 g/5 oz/1 cup roasted, unsalted peanuts
45 ml/3 tbsp vegetable oil
1 small onion, roughly chopped
2 garlic cloves, crushed
1 red chilli, seeded and chopped
2.5 cm/1 in piece root ginger, peeled and chopped
5 cm/2 in piece lemon grass, roughly chopped
2.5 ml/$\frac{1}{2}$ tsp ground cumin
45 ml/3 tbsp chopped fresh coriander stalks
15 ml/1 tbsp sesame oil
175 ml/6 fl oz/$\frac{3}{4}$ cup coconut milk
30 ml/2 tbsp thick soy sauce (kecap manis)
10 ml/2 tsp lime juice
salt and pepper
lime wedges and chives, to garnish

**1** Rub the husks from the peanuts in a clean tea towel.

**2** Grind to a smooth paste, with 30 ml/2 tbsp vegetable oil, in a blender or food processor. Set to one side.

**3** Place the next seven ingredients in the blender or food processor and process to a fairly smooth paste.

**4** Heat the remaining vegetable oil with the sesame oil in a small saucepan and add the onion paste. Cook over a low heat for about 10–15 minutes, stirring occasionally.

garlic
red chilli
limes
coconut milk
root ginger
vegetable oil
thick soy sauce
onion
ground cumin
lemon grass
sesame oil
unsalted peanuts
coriander

**5** Stir in the peanuts, coconut milk, soy sauce and lime juice, and keep stirring while it heats through.

**6** Adjust the seasoning, then pour into small bowls or saucers. Serve warm with grilled, skewered chicken or pork, or with small spicy meatballs, garnished with lime wedges and chives.

## Creamy Dill and Mustard Sauce

This sauce will give a tangy, Scandinavian flavour to grilled fish dishes.

*Serves 3-4*

INGREDIENTS

25 g/1 oz/2 tbsp butter
20 g/³/₄ oz/1¹/₂ tbsp plain flour
300 ml/¹/₂ pint/1¹/₄ cups hot fish stock
15 ml/1 tbsp white wine vinegar
45 ml/3 tbsp chopped fresh dill
15 ml/1 tbsp wholegrain mustard
10 ml/2 tsp granulated sugar
2 egg yolks
salt and pepper

*plain flour*

*granulated sugar*

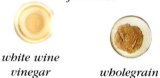
*dill*

*fish stock*

*white wine vinegar*

*wholegrain mustard*

*egg yolks*

*butter*

**1** Melt the butter and stir in the flour. Cook for 1–2 minutes over a low heat, stirring continuously.

**2** Remove from the heat and gradually blend in the hot stock. Return to the heat, bring to the boil, stirring all the time, then simmer for 2–3 minutes.

**3** Remove from the heat and beat in the vinegar, dill, mustard and sugar.

**4** Using a fork, beat the yolks in a small bowl and gradually add a small quantity of hot sauce. Return to the pan, whisking vigorously. Continue whisking over a very low heat for a further minute. Serve with grilled fillets of sole, plaice or brill.

# Orange and Caper Sauce

A wonderfully sweet-sour sauce to add zest to otherwise plain white fish.

*Serves 3-4*

INGREDIENTS
25 g/1 oz/2 tbsp butter
1 onion, chopped
fish bones and trimmings
5 ml/1 tsp black peppercorns
300 ml/½ pint/1¼ cups dry
   white wine
2 small oranges
15 ml/1 tbsp capers, drained
60 ml/4 tbsp crème fraîche
salt and pepper

*fish bones and trimmings*

*onion*

*crème fraîche*

*dry white wine*

*butter*

*black peppercorns*

*oranges*

*capers*

**1** Melt the butter and add the onion. Sauté over a moderate heat until the onion is lightly browned.

**2** Add the fish trimmings and peppercorns, and pour in the wine. Cover and simmer gently for 30 minutes.

**3** Using a serrated knife, peel the oranges, ensuring all the white pith is removed. Ease the segments away from the membrane.

**4** Strain the stock into a clean saucepan. Add the capers and orange segments together with any juice and heat through. Lower the heat and gently stir in the crème fraîche and seasoning. Serve hot with grilled or poached skate wings or plaice.

# Watercress Cream

The delicate green colour of this cream sauce looks wonderful against pink-fleshed fish like salmon or salmon trout.

*Serves 4*

INGREDIENTS
2 bunches watercress
25 g/1 oz/2 tbsp butter
2 shallots, chopped
25 g/1 oz/2 tbsp plain flour
150 ml/¼ pint/⅔ cup hot fish stock
150 ml/¼ pint/⅔ cup dry white wine
5 ml/1 tsp anchovy essence
150 ml/¼ pint/⅔ cup single cream
salt
pinch cayenne pepper
lemon juice

*anchovy essence*

*watercress*

*plain flour*

*shallots*

*single cream*

*cayenne pepper*

*dry white wine*

*fish stock*

*butter*

**1** Trim the watercress of any bruised leaves and coarse stalks. Blanch in boiling water for 5 minutes.

**2** Drain and refresh the watercress under cold running water. In a sieve, press well with the back of a kitchen spoon to remove excess moisture then chop finely.

**3** Melt the butter and fry the shallots until soft. Stir in the flour and cook for 1–2 minutes.

**4** Turn off the heat and gradually blend in the stock, followed by the wine. Return to the heat, bring to the boil, stirring continuously, and simmer gently for 2–3 minutes.

## VARIATION

To make rocket cream sauce, replace the watercress with 25 g/1 oz rocket leaves.

**5** Strain into a clean pan, then add the watercress, anchovy essence and cream. Warm through over a low heat.

**6** Season with salt and cayenne pepper and sharpen with lemon juice to taste. Serve immediately with grilled or poached salmon.

# Garlic and Chilli Dip

This dip is delicious with fresh prawns and other shellfish. It will also spice up any kind of fish when used as an accompanying sauce.

*Serves 4*

INGREDIENTS
1 small red chilli
2.5 cm/1 in piece root ginger
2 garlic cloves
5 ml/1 tsp mustard powder
15 ml/1 tbsp chilli sauce
30 ml/2 tbsp olive oil
30 ml/2 tbsp light soy sauce
juice of two limes
30 ml/2 tbsp chopped fresh
   parsley
salt and pepper

*mustard powder*   *red chilli*   *parsley*

*root ginger*

*light soy sauce*

*chilli sauce*   *limes*

*garlic*

**1** Halve the chilli, remove the seeds, stalk and membrane, and chop finely. Peel and roughly chop the ginger.

**2** Crush the chilli, ginger, garlic and mustard powder to a paste, using a pestle and mortar.

**3** In a bowl, mix together all the remaining ingredients, except the parsley Add the paste and blend it in. Cover and chill for 24 hours.

**4** Stir in the parsley and season to taste. It is best to serve in small individual bowls for dipping.

## COOK'S TIP

Medium-sized Mediterranean prawns are ideal served with this sauce. Remove the shell but leave the tails intact so there is something to hold on to.

# Saffron Cream

The subtle flavour and colouring of this sauce marries well with steamed or pan-fried scallops in a freshly-baked vol-au-vent.

*Serves 4*

INGREDIENTS
pinch saffron threads
30 ml/2 tbsp hot water
25 g/1 oz/2 tbsp butter
2 shallots, finely chopped
90 ml/6 tbsp dry white wine
60 ml/4 tbsp double cream
1 quantity fish Velouté Sauce, hot
2 egg yolks
salt and pepper
fresh chervil, to garnish

*double cream*    *egg yolks*

*butter*

*Velouté Sauce*

*shallots*

*saffron threads*

*dry white wine*

**1** Soak the saffron threads in the water for 15 minutes.

**2** Melt the butter and sauté the shallots until softened, add the wine and simmer gently until reduced by half.

**3** Strain in the saffron water and add the cream, and cook very gently for about 2 minutes.

**4** Blend the egg yolks with a little hot Velouté Sauce and, off the heat, whisk with the remaining sauce into the wine and cream. Season lightly.

# Maître d'Hôtel Butter

Some fish have such a delicate flavour it's a pity to mask it with heavy sauces. This butter, and the variations below, make subtle accompaniments.

*Serves 4-6*

INGREDIENTS

115 g/4 oz/$\frac{1}{2}$ cup softened
   butter
30 ml/2 tbsp parsley, finely
   chopped
2.5 ml/$\frac{1}{2}$ tsp lemon juice
cayenne pepper
salt and pepper

*parsley*

*lemon*

*cayenne pepper*

*butter*

**1**  Beat the butter until creamy then beat in the parsley, lemon juice and cayenne pepper, and season lightly.

**2**  Spread the butter 1 cm/$\frac{1}{4}$ in thick on to aluminium foil, chill then cut into shapes with a knife or fancy cutter.

## VARIATIONS

**LEMON AND LIME BUTTER**
Add 15 ml/1 tbsp finely grated lemon or lime rind and 15 ml/1 tbsp juice to the butter.

**HERB BUTTER**
Replace the parsley with 30 ml/ 2 tbsp chopped mint, chives or tarragon.

**GARLIC BUTTER**
Add 2 skinned and crushed cloves of garlic to the softened butter with 15–30 ml/1–2 tbsp chopped parsley.

**ANCHOVY BUTTER**
Add 6 anchovy fillets, drained of oil and mashed with a fork, to the softened butter. Season with pepper only.

**MUSTARD BUTTER**
Add 10 ml/2 tsp English mustard and 30 ml/2 tbsp chopped chives to the butter.

**3**  Alternatively, form into a roll, wrap in clear film or aluminium foil and chill. Cut off slices as required.

## COOK'S TIP
These butters will keep in the fridge for several days, and will also freeze, but make sure you wrap them well to avoid any loss of flavour.

## Pesto Sauce

There is nothing more evocative of the warmth of Italy than a good home-made pesto. Serve generous spoonfuls with your favourite pasta.

*Serves 3-4*

INGREDIENTS
50 g/2 oz/2 cups tightly packed
    basil leaves
2 garlic cloves, crushed
30 ml/2 tbsp pine nuts
120 ml/4 fl oz/1/2 cup olive oil
40 g/11/2 oz/2/3 cup Parmesan
    cheese, finely grated
salt and pepper

*garlic*

*Parmesan cheese*

*pine nuts*

*olive oil*

*basil*

**1** Using a pestle and mortar, grind the basil, garlic, pine nuts and seasoning to a fine paste.

**2** Transfer the mixture to a bowl and whisk in the oil a little at a time.

**3** Add the cheese and blend well. Adjust the seasoning to taste.

**4** Alternatively, place the basil, garlic, pine nuts and seasoning in a food processor and grind as finely as possible.

**5** With the food processor on, slowly add the oil in a thin stream to give a smooth paste.

**6** Add the cheese and pulse quickly 3–4 times. Adjust the seasoning if necessary and heat gently.

## VARIATION
Pesto also makes an excellent dressing on small new potatoes. Serve while still hot or allow to cool to room temperature.

# Rich Tomato Sauce

For a full tomato flavour and rich red colour use only really ripe tomatoes. Fresh plum tomatoes are an excellent choice if you can find them.

*Serves 4-6*

INGREDIENTS
30 ml/2 tbsp olive oil
1 large onion, chopped
2 garlic cloves, crushed
1 carrot, finely chopped
1 celery stick, finely chopped
675 g/1½ lb tomatoes, peeled and chopped
150 ml/¼ pint/²/₃ cup red wine
150 ml/¼ pint/²/₃ cup vegetable stock
1 bouquet garni
15 ml/1 tbsp tomato purée
2.5-5 ml/½-1 tsp granulated sugar
salt and pepper

vegetable stock

onion

carrot

red wine

olive oil

garlic

tomato purée

tomatoes

celery

bouquet garni

**1** Heat the oil and sauté the onion and garlic until soft. Add the carrot and celery and continue to cook, stirring occasionally, until golden.

**2** Stir in the tomatoes, wine, stock, bouquet garni and seasoning. Bring to the boil, cover and simmer for 45 minutes, stirring occasionally.

**3** Remove the bouquet garni and adjust the seasoning, adding sugar and tomato purée as necessary.

**4** Serve the sauce as it is or, for a smoother texture, purée in a blender or food processor, or press through a sieve. Spoon over sliced courgettes or whole round beans.

# Gorgonzola & Walnut Sauce

This is a very quick but indulgently creamy sauce. Serve with pasta and a green salad for a delicious lunch or supper.

### Serves 2

INGREDIENTS

50 g/2 oz/4 tbsp butter
50 g/2 oz button mushrooms, sliced
150 g/5 oz Gorgonzola cheese
150 ml/¼ pint/⅔ cup soured cream
salt and pepper
25 g/1 oz Pecorino cheese, grated
50 g/2 oz/½ cup broken walnut pieces

*soured cream*

*walnuts*

*button mushrooms*

*Pecorino cheese*

*Gorgonzola cheese*

**1** Melt the butter and gently fry the mushrooms until lightly browned.

**2** With a fork, mash together the Gorgonzola, cream and seasoning.

**3** Stir in the mushroom mixture and heat gently until melted.

**4** Finally stir in the Pecorino cheese and the walnut pieces.

## COOK'S TIP

For an impressive vegetable dish, layer with lightly cooked, thickly sliced potatoes. Sprinkle with more Pecorino cheese and bake at 180°C/350°F/Gas 4 for 1 hour.

# Sweet Pepper & Chilli Sauce

A mellow, warming sauce, ideal with pasta. For a more extravagant supper dish add thickly sliced chorizo sausage with the sun-dried tomatoes.

*Serves 3-4*

INGREDIENTS
30 ml/2 tbsp olive oil
1 onion, chopped
1 garlic clove, crushed
2 large red or orange peppers, seeded and finely chopped
5 ml/1 tsp chilli seasoning
15 ml/1 tbsp paprika
2.5 ml/¹/₂ tsp dried thyme
1 x 225 g/8 oz can chopped tomatoes
300 ml/¹/₂ pint/1¹/₄ cups vegetable stock
2.5 ml/¹/₂ tsp granulated sugar
salt and pepper
30 ml/2 tbsp sun-dried tomatoes in oil, drained and chopped

onion
olive oil
garlic
red pepper
paprika
thyme
chopped tomatoes

sun-dried tomatoes

**1** Heat the oil and sauté the onion, garlic and peppers for 4–5 minutes or until lightly browned.

**2** Add the chilli, paprika and thyme and cook for a further minute.

**3** Stir in the tomatoes, stock, sugar and seasoning, and bring to the boil. Cover and simmer for 30 minutes or until soft, adding more stock if necessary.

**4** Ten minutes before the end of cooking, add the sun-dried tomatoes. Serve hot with freshly cooked pasta.

# Spicy Tuna Dip

A piquant dip, delicious with breadsticks – use more oil for a sauce, less for filling hard-boiled eggs, tomatoes or celery sticks.

*Serves 6*

INGREDIENTS
1 x 90g/3½ oz can tuna fish in oil
olive oil
4 hard-boiled eggs
75 g/3 oz stoned green olives
1 x 50 g/2 oz can anchovy fillets, drained
45 ml/3 tbsp capers, drained
10 ml/2 tsp Dijon mustard
pepper
parsley, to garnish

*tuna*

*eggs*

*anchovy fillets*

*green olives*

*olive oil*

*Dijon mustard*

**1** Drain the tuna and make up the oil to 90 ml/6 tbsp with olive oil.

**2** Halve the hard-boiled eggs, remove the yolks and then place in a blender or food processor. Discard the whites.

**3** Reserve a few olives for garnishing, then add the rest to the blender together with the remaining ingredients. Whizz together until smooth. Season with pepper to taste.

**4** Spoon into a bowl and garnish with the reserved olives and parsley. Serve with bread sticks for dipping.

# Mousseline Sauce

A truly luscious sauce, subtly flavoured, rich and creamy.

*Serves 4*

INGREDIENTS
1 quantity Hollandaise sauce
*or* for a less rich sauce:
  2 egg yolks
  15 ml/1 tbsp lemon juice
  75 g/3 oz/6 tbsp softened
  butter
90 ml/6 tbsp double cream
salt and pepper

*butter*

*lemon*

*double cream*

*egg yolks*

**1** If you are not using prepared Hollandaise, make the sauce; whisk the yolks and lemon juice in a bowl over a pan of barely simmering water until very thick and fluffy.

**2** Whisk in the butter, but only a very little at a time, until it is thoroughly absorbed and the sauce has the consistency of mayonnaise.

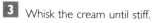

**3** Whisk the cream until stiff.

**4** Fold into the warm Hollandaise or prepared sauce and adjust the seasoning. You can add a little more lemon juice for extra sharpness. Serve as a dip with prepared artichokes or artichoke hearts.

# Walnut Sauce with Tagliatelle

**An unusual sauce which would make this a spectacular dinner party starter.**

*Serves 4–6*

INGREDIENTS

2 thick slices wholemeal (whole-
   wheat) bread
300 ml/10 fl oz/1¼ cups milk
275 g/10 oz/2½ cups walnut pieces
1 garlic clove, crushed
50 g/2 oz/½ cup freshly grated
   Parmesan cheese
90 ml/6 tbsp olive oil, plus extra for
   tossing the pasta
salt and pepper
150 ml/5 fl oz/⅓ cup double (heavy)
   cream (optional)
450 g/1 lb tagliatelle
30 ml/2 tbsp chopped fresh parsley

**1** Cut the crusts off the bread and soak in the milk until the milk is all absorbed.

**2** Pre-heat the oven to 190°C/375°F/ gas mark 5. Spread the walnuts on a baking sheet and toast in the oven for 5 minutes. Leave to cool.

**3** Place the bread, walnuts, garlic, Parmesan cheese and olive oil in a food processor and blend until smooth. Season to taste with salt and pepper. Stir in the cream, if using.

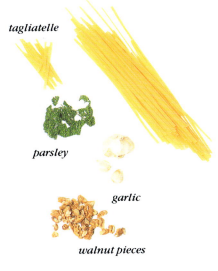

*tagliatelle*

*parsley*

*garlic*

*walnut pieces*

**4** Cook the pasta in plenty of boiling salted water, drain and toss with a little olive oil. Divide the pasta equally between 4 bowls and place a dollop of sauce on each portion. Sprinkle with parsley.

## VARIATION

Add 100 g/4 oz/¾ cup stoned (pitted) black olives to the food processor with the other ingredients for a richer, more piquant sauce. The Greek-style olives have the most flavour.

# Tomato and Clam Sauce with Spaghetti

Small sweet clams make this a delicately succulent sauce. Cockles would make a good substitute, or even mussels. Don't be tempted to use seafood pickled in vinegar – the result will be inedible!

*Serves 4*

INGREDIENTS

900 g/2 lb live small clams, or 2 × 400 g/14 oz cans clams in brine, drained
90 ml/6 tbsp olive oil
2 garlic cloves, crushed
600 g/1 lb 5 oz canned chopped tomatoes
45 ml/3 tbsp chopped fresh parsley
salt and pepper
450 g/1 lb spaghetti

*olive oil*          *spaghetti*

*parsley*

*garlic*

*clams*

**1** If using live clams, place them in a bowl of cold water and rinse several times to remove any grit or sand. Drain.

**2** Heat the oil in a saucepan and add the clams. Stir over a high heat until the clams open. Throw away any that do not open. Transfer the clams to a bowl with a perforated spoon.

**3** Reduce the clam juice left in the pan to almost nothing by boiling fast; this will also concentrate the flavour. Add the garlic and fry until golden. Pour in the tomatoes, bring to the boil and cook for 3–4 minutes until reduced. Stir in the clam mixture or canned clams and half the parsley and heat through. Season.

**4** Cook the pasta in plenty of boiling salted water according to the manufacturer's instructions. Drain well and turn into a warm serving dish. Pour over the sauce and sprinkle with the remaining parsley.

# Creamy Gruyère Sauce

Gruyère gives this sauce a sweet nutty flavour and it melts wonderfully to a rich velvety smoothness.

*Serves 6*

INGREDIENTS

40 g/1½ oz/3 tbsp butter
40 g/1½ oz/3 tbsp plain flour
450 ml/¾ pint/1⅞ cup hot
   vegetable or light stock
2 egg yolks
5 ml/1 tsp Dijon mustard
pinch of ground mace
30 ml/2 tbsp dry sherry
75 g/3 oz Gruyère cheese, grated

*vegetable stock*

*dry sherry*

*ground mace*

*Gruyère cheese*

*butter*

*egg yolks*

*plain flour*

*Dijon mustard*

**1** Melt the butter and stir in the flour, and cook over a moderate heat for about 1–2 minutes.

**2** Remove from the heat and gradually blend in the hot stock. Return to the heat and bring to the boil, stirring continuously until the sauce thickens. Simmer gently for 3–4 minutes.

**3** In a small bowl, blend the egg yolks with a little hot sauce.

**4** Return to the pan and cook over a very low heat for 1–2 minutes. Do not allow to boil. Finally stir in the flavourings and cheese. Season to taste. Serve with steamed broccoli, cauliflower or leeks.

## COOK'S TIP

Crisply fried buttered crumbs and flaked or nibbed almonds may be sprinkled over for added crunch.

## How to Marinate

Marinades are used to add flavour, moisten or tenderize foods, particularly meat. Marinades can be either savoury or sweet and are as varied as you want to make them; spicy, fruity, fragrant or exotic. Certain classic combinations always work well with certain foods. Usually, it's best to choose oily marinades for dry foods, such as lean meat or white fish, and wine- or vinegar-based marinades for rich foods with a higher fat content. Most marinades don't contain salt, which can draw out the juices from meat; it's best to add salt just before cooking.

**1** Place the food for marinating in a wide dish or bowl, preferably large enough to allow it to lie in a single layer.

**2** Mix together the ingredients for the marinade thoroughly.

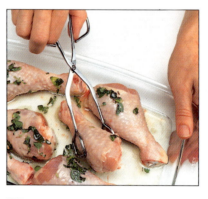

**3** Pour the marinade over the food and turn the food, to coat it evenly.

**4** Cover the dish and refrigerate from 30 minutes up to several hours, depending on the recipe, turning the food over occasionally, and spooning the marinade over it.

**5** Remove the food with a slotted spoon, or lift it out with tongs, and drain off and reserve the marinade. If necessary, allow the food to come to room temperature before cooking.

**6** Use the marinade for basting or brushing the food, during cooking.

# Marinades For Barbecues

## BASIC BARBECUE MARINADE

This can be used for meat or fish.

1 garlic clove, crushed
45 ml/3 tbsp sunflower or
  olive oil
45 ml/3 tbsp dry sherry
15 ml/1 tbsp Worcestershire
  sauce
15 ml/1 tbsp dark soy sauce
freshly ground black pepper

## HERB MARINADE

This is good for fish, meat or poultry.

120 ml/4 fl oz/$\frac{1}{2}$ cup dry white wine
60 ml/4 tbsp olive oil
15 ml/1 tbsp lemon juice
30 ml/2 tbsp finely chopped fresh
  herbs, such as parsley, thyme,
  chives or basil
freshly ground black pepper

## COOK'S TIP

The amount of marinade you will need depends on the amount of the food but, as a rough guide, about 150 ml/$\frac{1}{4}$ pint/$\frac{2}{3}$ cup is enough for about 500 g/1$\frac{1}{4}$ lb of food.

## HONEY CITRUS MARINADE

This is good with fish or chicken.

finely grated rind and juice of
  $\frac{1}{2}$ lime, $\frac{1}{2}$ lemon and $\frac{1}{2}$ small
  orange
45 ml/3 tbsp sunflower oil
30 ml/2 tbsp clear honey
15 ml/1 tbsp soy sauce
5 ml/1 tsp Dijon mustard
freshly ground black pepper

## YOGURT SPICE MARINADE

For fish, meats or poultry.

150 ml/$\frac{1}{4}$ pint/$\frac{2}{3}$ cup natural
  yogurt
1 small onion, finely chopped
1 garlic clove, crushed
5 ml/1 tsp finely chopped fresh
  root ginger
5 ml/1 tsp ground coriander
5 ml/1 tsp ground cumin
2.5 ml/$\frac{1}{2}$ tsp ground turmeric

## RED WINE MARINADE

Good with red meats and game.

150 ml/$\frac{1}{4}$ pint/$\frac{2}{3}$ cup dry red
  wine
15 ml/1 tbsp olive oil
15 ml/1 tbsp red-wine vinegar
2 garlic cloves, crushed
2 dried bay leaves, crumbled
freshly ground black pepper

# Red Wine and Juniper Marinade

Marinating develops a rich base for casseroles and stews. This marinade is also excellent for pot-roasted beef.

*Serves 4-6*

INGREDIENTS
700 g/1¹/₂ lb boned leg of lamb, trimmed and cut into 2.5 cm/ 1 in cubes

FOR THE MARINADE:
2 carrots, cut into batons
225 g/8 oz baby onions or shallots
100 g/4 oz button mushrooms
4 rosemary sprigs
8 juniper berries, lightly crushed
8 black peppercorns, lightly crushed
300 ml/¹/₂ pint/1¹/₄ cups red wine
30 ml/2 tbsp vegetable oil
150 ml/¹/₄ pint/²/₃ cup stock
30 ml/2 tbsp beurre manié

**1** Place the meat in a bowl, add the vegetables, rosemary and spices then pour over the wine. Cover and leave in a cool place for 4-5 hours, stirring once or twice during this time.

**2** Remove the lamb and vegetables with a slotted spoon and set aside. Strain the marinade into a jug.

**3** Preheat the oven to 170°C/325°F/Gas 3. Heat the oil in a pan and fry the meat and vegetables in batches until lightly browned. Pour over the reserved marinade and stock. Cover and cook in the oven for 2 hours.

*red wine*

*baby onions*

*juniper berries and black peppercorns*

*button mushrooms*

*carrot*

*rosemary*

**4** Twenty minutes before the end of cooking stir in the beurre manié, cover and return to the oven. Season to taste before serving.

# Chinese-style Marinade with Toasted Sesame Seeds

Toasted sesame seeds bring their distinctive smoky aroma to this Oriental marinade.

*Serves 4*

INGREDIENTS
450 g/1 lb rump steak
30 ml/2 tbsp sesame seeds
15 ml/1 tbsp sesame oil
30 ml/2 tbsp vegetable oil
100 g/4 oz small mushrooms, quartered
1 large green pepper, seeded and diced
4 spring onions, chopped diagonally

FOR THE MARINADE:
10 ml/2 tsp cornflour
30 ml/2 tbsp rice wine or sherry
15 ml/1 tbsp lemon juice
15 ml/1 tbsp soy sauce
few drops Tabasco sauce
2.5 cm/1 in piece root ginger, peeled and grated
1 garlic clove, crushed

lemon

soy sauce

sesame oil

sherry

Tabasco sauce

cornflour

garlic

sesame seeds

root ginger

**1** Trim the steak and cut into thin strips about 1 cm x 5 cm/¹⁄₂ x 2 in.

**2** In a bowl, blend the cornflour with the sherry then stir in the other marinade ingredients. Stir in the beef strips, cover and leave in a cool place for 3-4 hours.

**3** Place the sesame seeds in a large frying pan or wok. Cook dry over a moderate heat, shaking the pan until the seeds are golden. Reserve on one side.

**4** Heat the oils in the frying pan. Drain the beef, reserving the marinade, and brown a few pieces at a time. Remove with a slotted spoon.

**VARIATION**
This marinade would also be good with pork or chicken.

**5**   Add the mushrooms and pepper and fry for 2–3 minutes, moving the vegetables continuously.  Add the spring onions and cook for a further minute.

**6**   Return the beef with the marinade and stir over a moderate heat for a further 2 minutes until the ingredients are evenly coated with glaze. Just before serving, sprinkle with sesame seeds.

# Summer Herb Marinade

Make the best use of summer herbs in this marinade, which is designed for the barbecue. Any combination may be used depending on what you have to hand, and it can be used with veal, chicken, pork, salmon or lamb.

*Serves 4*

INGREDIENTS
4 pieces of meat or fish

FOR THE MARINADE:
fresh herb sprigs, e.g. chervil,
 thyme, parsley, sage, chives,
 rosemary, oregano
90 ml/6 tbsp olive oil
45 ml/3 tbsp tarragon vinegar
1 garlic clove, crushed
2 spring onions, chopped
salt and pepper

*parsley*  *chervil*  *garlic*  *tarragon vinegar*  *olive oil*  *spring onions*  *chives*  *thyme*  *rosemary*  *oregano*

**1** Discard any coarse stalks or damaged leaves from the herbs, then chop very finely.

**2** Mix the herbs with the remaining marinade ingredients.

**3** Place the meat or fish in a bowl and pour over the marinade. Cover and leave in a cool place for 4–6 hours.

**4** Brush the pieces of meat or fish with the marinade and cook under a hot grill or over a barbecue, turning occasionally until they are tender. Baste with the marinade while they cook. Serve garnished with fresh herbs.

# Ginger and Lime Marinade

This fragrant marinade will guarantee a mouth-watering aroma from the barbecue, and is as delicious with chicken or pork as it is with fish.

*Serves 4-6*

INGREDIENTS
FOR THE KEBABS:
500 g/1¼ lb prawns and cubed monkfish
selection of prepared vegetables, e.g. red, green or orange peppers, courgettes, button mushrooms, red onion, bay leaves, cherry tomtoes

FOR THE MARINADE:
3 limes
15 ml/1 tbsp green cardamom pods
1 onion, finely chopped
2.5 cm/1 in piece root ginger, peeled and grated
1 large garlic clove,crushed
45 ml/3 tbsp olive oil

*root ginger*

*onion*

*garlic*

*limes*

*olive oil*

*green cardamoms*

**1** Finely grate the rind from one lime and squeeze the juice from all of them.

**2** Split the cardamom pods and remove the seeds. Crush with a pestle and mortar or the back of a heavy-bladed knife.

**3** Mix all the marinade ingredients together and pour over the meat or fish. Stir in gently, cover and leave in a cool place for 2–3 hours.

**4** Thread four skewers alternately with fish and vegetables. Cook slowly under a hot grill or over a barbecue, basting occasionally with the marinade.

# Spicy Yogurt Marinade

Plan this dish well in advance; the extra-long marinating time is necessary to develop a really mellow spicy flavour.

*Serves 6*

INGREDIENTS
6 chicken pieces
juice of 1 lemon
5 ml/1 tsp salt

FOR THE MARINADE:
5 ml/1 tsp coriander seeds
10 ml/2 tsp cumin seeds
6 cloves
2 bay leaves
1 onion, quartered
2 garlic cloves
5 cm/2 in piece root ginger, peeled and roughly chopped
2.5 ml/¹⁄₂ tsp chilli powder
5 ml/1 tsp turmeric
150 ml/¹⁄₄ pint/²⁄₃ cup natural yogurt
lemon, lime or coriander, to garnish

*yogurt*  *lemon*
*root ginger*  *coriander seeds*
*onion*
*garlic*  *bay leaves*
*chilli powder*
*turmeric*
*cloves*  *cumin seeds*

## VARIATION
This marinade will also work well brushed over skewers of lamb or pork fillet.

**1** Skin the chicken joints and make deep slashes in the fleshiest parts with a sharp knife. Sprinkle over the lemon and salt and rub in.

**2** Spread the coriander and cumin seeds, cloves and bay leaves in the bottom of a large frying pan and dry-fry over a moderate heat until the bay leaves are crispy.

**3** Cool the spices and grind coarsely with a pestle and mortar.

**4** Finely mince the onion, garlic and ginger in a food processor or blender. Add the ground spices, chilli, turmeric and yogurt, then strain in the lemon juice from the chicken.

**5** Arrange the chicken in a single layer in a roasting tin. Pour over the marinade, then cover and chill for 24–36 hours.

**6** Occasionally turn the chicken pieces in the marinade. Preheat the oven to 200°C/400°F/Gas 6. Cook the chicken for 45 minutes. Serve hot or cold, garnished with fresh leaves and slices of lemon or lime.

# Winter Spiced Ale Marinade

Serve this on frosty evenings with buttered rutabagas and crisply cooked cabbage. This marinade can also be used in a casserole of beef or lamb pieces.

*Serves 6*

INGREDIENTS
3 lb top round beef

FOR THE MARINADE:
1 onion, sliced
2 carrots, sliced
2 celery stalks, sliced
2–3 parsley stalks, lightly crushed
large fresh thyme sprig
2 bay leaves
6 cloves, lightly crushed
1 cinnamon stick
8 black peppercorns
1¼ cups dark ale
3 tbsp vegetable oil
2 tbsp beurre manié
salt and pepper

carrot
parsley
vegetable oil
beurre manié
cinnamon
cloves and black peppercorns
thyme
onion
dark ale
bay leaves
celery

**1** Place the meat in a plastic bag placed inside a large deep bowl. Add the vegetables, herbs and spices, then pour over the ale. Seal the bag and leave in a cool place for 5–6 hours.

**2** Remove the beef and set aside. Strain the marinade into a bowl, reserving the vegetables.

**3** Heat the oil in a flame-proof casserole. Fry the vegetables until lightly browned, then remove with a slotted spoon and set aside. Brown the beef all over in the remaining oil.

**4** Preheat the oven to 325°F. Pour over the reserved marinade and return the vegetables to the casserole. Cover the casserole and cook for 2½ hours. Turn the beef 2 or 3 times in the marinade during this time.

**5** To serve, remove the beef and slice neatly. Arrange on a plate with the vegetables. Stir the beurre manié into the marinade and bring to a boil. Adjust the seasoning before serving.

# Rosemary Marinade

If you are serving lamb for your Sunday roast, marinate overnight in the fridge.

*Serves 6*

INGREDIENTS
1.5 kg/3-3½ lb leg of lamb
2 garlic cloves, sliced

FOR THE MARINADE:
1 lemon, sliced
6 rosemary sprigs
4 lemon thyme sprigs
300 ml/½ pint/1¼ cups dry
   white wine
60 ml/4 tbsp olive oil
salt and pepper
15 ml/1 tbsp cornflour

*rosemary*  *lemon thyme*

*lemon*

*olive oil*  *dry white wine*

*garlic*

**1** Make small cuts over the surface of the lamb and insert a slice of garlic in each, so they sit proud.

**2** Place the lamb in a roasting tin, with the lemon slices and herbs scattered over it. Mix the remaining marinade ingredients and pour over the joint. Cover and leave in a cool place for 4–6 hours, turning occasionally. Preheat the oven to 180°C/350°F/Gas 4. Roast the lamb for 25 minutes per 450 g/1 lb plus 25 minutes over.

**3** When the lamb is cooked, transfer to a warmed plate to rest. Drain the excess fat from the pan. Blend the cornflour with a little cold water and stir into the juices, stir over a moderate heat for 2–3 minutes and season to taste.

## VARIATION
You can also use lemon and rosemary marinade for chicken pieces, but you must roast the meat without the marinade because otherwise it will become tough. Use the marinade for making into gravy when the chicken is cooked.

# Orange and Green Peppercorn Marinade

This is an excellent light marinade for whole fish. The mouth-watering beauty of a whole fish and the soft-coloured marinade needs only a sprig of fresh herb to garnish.

*Serves 4*

INGREDIENTS
1 medium-sized whole fish, e.g. salmon trout, bass or sea bream, cleaned

FOR THE MARINADE:
1 red onion
2 small oranges
90 ml/6 tbsp light olive oil
30 ml/2 tbsp cider vinegar
30 ml/2 tbsp green peppercorns in brine, drained
30 ml/2 tbsp chopped fresh parsley
salt and sugar

*oranges*

*red onion*

*cider vinegar*

*parsley*

*green peppercorns*

*light olive oil*

**1** With a sharp knife, slash the fish 3–4 times on both sides.

**2** Line an ovenproof dish with foil. Peel and slice the onion and oranges. Lay half in the bottom of the dish, place the fish on top, and cover with the remaining onion and orange.

**3** Mix the remaining marinade ingredients and pour over the fish. Cover and stand for 4 hours, occasionally spooning the marinade over the top.

**4** Preheat the oven to 180°C/350°F/Gas 4. Fold up the aluminium foil over the fish and seal loosely. Bake for 15 minutes per 450 g/1 lb, plus 15 minutes over.

# SALSAS

## Tomato Salsas

Salsa is Spanish for sauce, but elsewhere it has come to mean a side dish of finely chopped vegetables or fruits, which really enhances the meals it accompanies.

### Serves 6

INGREDIENTS
6 medium tomatoes
1 green Kenyan chilli
2 spring onions, chopped
10 cm/4 in length cucumber, diced
30 ml/2 tbsp lemon juice
30 ml/2 tbsp fresh coriander, chopped
15 ml/1 tbsp fresh parsley, chopped
salt and pepper

basil

tomatoes

orange pepper

parsley

lemon

spring onions

coriander

garlic

cucumber

capers

green Kenyan chilli

**1** Cut a small cross in the stalk end of each tomato. Place in a bowl and cover with boiling water.

**2** After 30 seconds or as soon as the skins split, drain and plunge into cold water. Gently slide off the skins. Quarter the tomatoes, remove the seeds and dice the flesh.

**3** Halve the chilli, remove the stalk, seeds and membrane, and chop finely.

**4** Mix together all the ingredients and transfer to a serving bowl. Chill for 1–2 hours before serving.

## VARIATIONS

Tomato and Caper Salsa: Prepare the tomatoes and stir in the onion and lemon juice. Add six torn sprigs of basil and 15 ml/1 tbsp roughly chopped capers. Season to taste.

Tomato and Roast Pepper Salsa: Prepare 4 tomatoes and stir in the chilli, onion and herbs. Add a roasted, peeled and diced orange pepper and a crushed garlic clove. Season to taste.

# Chilli and Coconut Salsa

A sweet-sour salsa that goes well with grilled or barbecued fish.

*Serves 6-8*

INGREDIENTS
1 small coconut
1 small pineapple
2 green Kenyan chillies
5 cm/2 in piece lemon grass
60 ml/4 tbsp natural yogurt
2.5 ml/$\frac{1}{2}$ tsp salt
30 ml/2 tbsp chopped coriander
coriander sprigs, to garnish

*green chillies*

*coconut*

*lemon grass*

*yogurt*

*pineapple*

*coriander*

**1** Puncture two of the coconut eyes with a screwdriver and drain the milk out from the shell.

**2** Crack the shell, prise away the flesh, and coarsely grate the coconut into a bowl.

**3** Cut the rind from the pineapple with a sharp knife and remove the eyes with a potato peeler. Finely chop the flesh and add to the coconut together with any juice.

**4** Halve the chillies lengthways and remove the stalks, seeds and membrane. Chop very finely and stir into the coconut mixture.

**5** Finely chop the lemon grass with a very sharp knife. Add to the coconut mixture and stir in.

**6** Add the remaining ingredients and stir well. Spoon into a serving dish and garnish with coriander sprigs.

# Roasted Pepper and Ginger Salsa

Char-grilling to remove the skins will take away any bitterness from the peppers.

*Serves 6*

INGREDIENTS
1 large red pepper
1 large yellow pepper
1 large orange pepper
2.5 cm/1 in piece root ginger
2.5 ml/$\frac{1}{2}$ tsp coriander seeds
5 ml/1 tsp cumin seeds
1 small garlic clove
30 ml/2 tbsp lime or lemon juice
1 small red onion, finely chopped
30 ml/2 tbsp chopped fresh
  coriander
5 ml/1 tsp chopped fresh thyme
salt and pepper

red pepper

thyme

yellow pepper

coriander and cumin seeds

orange pepper

garlic

lime

root ginger

coriander

## VARIATION
For a spicier version of this recipe, add a green chilli, finely chopped, to the pestle and mortar when grinding the ginger and garlic. Or simply add a sprinkle of cayenne pepper to the finished dish before chilling.

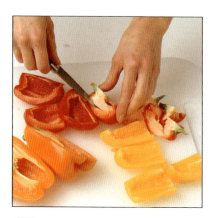

**1** Quarter the peppers and remove the stalk, seeds and membranes.

**2** Grill the quarters, skin side up, until charred and blistered. Rub away the skins and slice very finely.

**3** Peel or scrape the root ginger and chop roughly.

**4** Over a moderate heat, gently dry-fry the spices for 30 seconds to 1 minute, making sure they don't scorch.

**5** Crush the spices in a pestle and mortar. Add the ginger and garlic and continue to work to a pulp. Work in the lime or lemon juice.

**6** Mix together the peppers, spice mixture, onion and herbs. Season to taste and spoon into a serving bowl. Chill for 1–2 hours before serving as an accompaniment to barbecued meats or Halloumi cheese kebabs.

# Mango and Radish Salsa

The sweet flavour and juicy texture of mango in this salsa is contrasted very well by the hot and crunchy radishes. Simply serve with plain grilled fish or chicken.

## *Serves 4*

INGREDIENTS
1 large, ripe mango
12 radishes
juice of 1 lemon
45 ml/3 tbsp olive oil
red Tabasco sauce, to taste
45 ml/3 tbsp chopped fresh
  coriander
5 ml/1 tsp pink peppercorns
salt

TO SERVE
lettuce leaves
watercress sprigs
slices of seeded bread

mango

radishes

olive oil

lemon juice

red Tabasco sauce

coriander

pink peppercorns

**1** Holding the mango upright on a chopping board, use a large knife to slice the flesh away from either side of the large flat stone in two pieces. Using a smaller knife, carefully trim away any flesh still clinging to the top and bottom of the stone.

**2** Score the flesh of the mango halves deeply, taking care to avoid cutting through the skin: make parallel incisions about 1 cm/½ in apart; turn and cut lines in the opposite direction. Carefully turn the skin inside out so the flesh stands out like hedgehog spikes. Slice the diced flesh away from the skin.

**3** Trim the radishes, discarding the root tails and leaves. Coarsely grate the radishes or dice them finely and place in a bowl with the mango cubes.

**4** Stir the lemon juice and olive oil with salt and a few drops of Tabasco sauce to taste, then stir in the chopped coriander.

**5** Coarsely crush the pink peppercorns in a pestle and mortar or place them on a chopping board and flatten them with the heel of a heavy-bladed knife. Stir into the lemon oil.

**6** Toss the radishes and mango, pour in the dressing and toss again. Chill for up to 2 hours before serving.

## VARIATION
Try using papaya in place of the mango in this salsa.

# Guacamole

Nachos or tortilla chips are the perfect accompaniment for this classic Mexican dip.

## Serves 4

INGREDIENTS
2 ripe avocados
2 red chillies, seeded
1 garlic clove
1 shallot
30 ml/2 tbsp olive oil, plus extra
   to serve
juice of 1 lemon
salt
flat-leaf parsley leaves, to garnish

*avocados*

*red chillies*

*shallot*

*olive oil*

*garlic*

*lemon juice*

*flat-leaf parsley*

## VARIATION

Make a completely smooth guacamole by whizzing the ingredients in a blender or food processor. For a chunkier version, add a diced tomato or red pepper.

**1** Halve the avocados, remove their stones and, using a spoon, scoop out their flesh into a bowl.

**2** Mash the flesh well with a potato masher or a large fork.

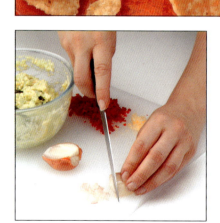

**3** Finely chop the chillies, garlic and shallot, then stir into the mashed avocado with the olive oil and lemon juice. Add salt to taste.

**4** Spoon the mixture into a small serving bowl. Drizzle over a little olive oil and scatter with a few flat-leaf parsley leaves. Serve immediately.

# Salsa Verde

There are many versions of this classic green salsa. Serve this one with creamy mashed potatoes or drizzled over chargrilled squid.

## Serves 4

INGREDIENTS

2–4 green chillies
8 spring onions
2 garlic cloves
50 g/2 oz salted capers
fresh tarragon sprig
bunch of fresh parsley
grated rind and juice of 1 lime
juice of 1 lemon
90 ml/6 tbsp olive oil
about 15 ml/1 tbsp green Tabasco
    sauce, to taste
black pepper

*chillies*

*spring onions*

*garlic*

*tarragon*

*capers*

*lime juice and grated lime rind*

*parsley*

*lemon juice*

*olive oil*

*green Tabasco sauce*

## VARIATION

If you can find only capers pickled in vinegar, they can be used for this salsa but must be rinsed well in cold water first.

**1** Halve the chillies and remove their seeds. Trim the spring onions and halve the garlic, then place in a food processor. Pulse the power briefly until all the ingredients are roughly chopped.

**2** Use your fingertips to rub the excess salt off the capers but do not rinse them (see Variation, below). Add the capers, tarragon and parsley to the food processor and pulse again until they are quite finely chopped.

**3** Transfer the mixture to a small bowl. Stir in the lime rind and juice, lemon juice and olive oil. Stir the mixture lightly so the citrus juice and oil do not emulsify.

**4** Add green Tabasco and black pepper to taste. Chill until ready to serve but do not prepare more than 8 hours in advance.

# Fiery Citrus Salsa

This very unusual salsa makes a fantastic marinade for shellfish and it is also delicious drizzled over barbecued meat.

*Serves 4*

INGREDIENTS
1 orange
1 green apple
2 fresh red chillies
1 garlic clove
8 fresh mint leaves
juice of 1 lemon
salt and pepper

*orange*          *apple*

*red chillies*       *garlic*

*mint*          *lemon juice*

**1** Slice the bottom off the orange so that it will stand firmly on a chopping board. Using a sharp knife, remove the peel by slicing from the top to the bottom of the orange.

**2** Hold the orange in one hand over a bowl. Slice towards the middle of the fruit, to one side of a segment, and then gently twist the knife to ease the segment away from the membrane and out of the orange. Repeat to remove all the segments. Squeeze any juice from the remaining membrane into the bowl.

**3** Peel the apple, slice it into wedges and remove the core.

**4** Halve the chillies and remove their seeds, then place them in a blender or food processor with the orange segments and juice, apple wedges, garlic and fresh mint.

**5** Process until smooth. Then, with the motor running, pour in the lemon juice.

**6** Season to taste with a little salt and pepper. Pour into a bowl or small jug and serve immediately.

## VARIATION
If you're feeling really fiery, don't seed the chillies! They will make the salsa particularly hot and fierce.

# Coriander Pesto Salsa

This aromatic salsa is delicious drizzled over fish and chicken, tossed with pasta ribbons or used to dress a fresh avocado and tomato salad. To transform it into a dip, mix it with a little mayonnaise or soured cream.

## Serves 4

INGREDIENTS
50 g/2 oz fresh coriander leaves
15 g/½ oz fresh parsley
2 red chillies
1 garlic clove
50 g/2 oz/⅓ cup shelled
    pistachio nuts
25 g/1 oz Parmesan cheese,
    finely grated
90 ml/6 tbsp olive oil
juice of 2 limes
salt and pepper

coriander

parsley

garlic

pistachio nuts

red chillies

olive oil

Parmesan cheese

lime juice

## VARIATION
Any number of different herbs or nuts may be used to make a similar salsa to this one – try a mixture of rosemary and parsley, or add a handful of black olives.

**1** Process the fresh coriander and parsley in a blender or food processor until finely chopped.

**2** Halve the chillies lengthways and remove their seeds. Add to the herbs together with the garlic and process until finely chopped.

**3** Add the pistachio nuts to the herb mixture and pulse the power until they are roughly chopped. Stir in the Parmesan cheese, olive oil and lime juice.

**4** Add salt and pepper, to taste. Spoon the mixture into a serving bowl and cover and chill until ready to serve.

# Feta and Olive Salsa

The salty flavour of the feta and olives in this chunky salsa is balanced by the bitter-tasting radicchio.

## Serves 4

INGREDIENTS

1 head of radicchio
250 g/9 oz feta cheese
150 g/5 oz black olives, halved and
    stoned
1 garlic clove
1 red chilli, seeded
45 ml/3 tbsp chopped fresh parsley
30 ml/2 tbsp olive oil
15 ml/1 tbsp balsamic vinegar
sea salt

*radicchio*

*feta cheese*

*black olives*

*garlic*

*red chilli*

*parsley*

*olive oil*

*balsamic vinegar*

**1** Separate the radicchio leaves and rinse them well in cold water. Roughly tear the leaves into small pieces.

**2** Cut or break the feta into small cubes. Place the radicchio in a bowl with the feta and olive halves and toss well to mix together.

## COOK'S TIP

Choose unpitted olives such as Kalamata for this salsa – they tend to have a stronger flavour and more interesting texture than the mild, pitted varieties.

**3** Finely chop the garlic and chilli, and sprinkle over the salsa with the chopped parsley, olive oil, balsamic vinegar and sea salt to taste.

**4** Mix together well, then transfer the salsa to a serving bowl and serve at room temperature.

# Chunky Cherry Tomato Salsa

Succulent cherry tomatoes and refreshing cucumber form the base of this delicious dill-seasoned salsa.

## Serves 4

INGREDIENTS
1 ridge cucumber
5 ml/1 tsp sea salt
500 g/1¼ lb cherry tomatoes
1 garlic clove
1 lemon
45 ml/3 tbsp chilli oil
2.5 ml/½ tsp dried chilli flakes
30 ml/2 tbsp chopped fresh dill
salt and pepper

ridge          cherry tomatoes
cucumber

chilli
flakes

fresh dill
chilli oil

lemon
garlic

**1** Trim the ends off the cucumber and cut it into 2.5 cm/1 in lengths, then cut each piece lengthways into thin slices.

**2** Arrange the cucumber slices in a colander and sprinkle them with the sea salt. Leave for 5 minutes until the cucumber has wilted.

**3** Wash the cucumber slices well under cold water and pat them dry with kitchen paper.

**4** Quarter the cherry tomatoes and place in a bowl with the wilted cucumber. Finely chop the garlic.

**5** Grate the lemon rind finely and place in a small jug with the juice from the lemon, the chilli oil, chilli flakes, dill and garlic. Add salt and pepper to taste, and whisk with a fork.

## VARIATION

Try flavouring this salsa with other fragrant herbs, such as tarragon, coriander or even mint.

**6** Pour the chilli oil dressing over the tomato and cucumber and toss well. Leave to marinate at room temperature for at least 2 hours before serving.

# Double Chilli Salsa

This is a scorchingly hot salsa for only the very brave! Spread it sparingly on to cooked meats and burgers.

## Serves 4–6

INGREDIENTS
6 habanero chillies or Scotch
  bonnets
2 ripe tomatoes
4 standard green jalapeño chillies
30 ml/2 tbsp chopped fresh parsley
30 ml/2 tbsp olive oil
15 ml/1 tbsp balsamic or sherry
  vinegar
salt

habanero
chillies

tomatoes

jalapeño
chillies

parsley

olive oil

balsamic
or sherry
vinegar

## VARIATION
Habanero chillies, or Scotch bonnets, are among the hottest fresh chillies available. You may prefer to tone down the heat of this salsa by using a milder variety.

**1** Skewer an habanero or Scotch bonnet chilli on a metal fork and hold it in a gas flame for 2–3 minutes, turning the chilli until the skin blackens and blisters. Repeat with all the chillies, then set aside.

**2** Skewer the tomatoes one at a time and hold in the flame for 1–2 minutes, until the skin splits and wrinkles. Slip off the skins, halve the tomatoes, then use a teaspoon to scoop out and discard the seeds. Chop the flesh very finely.

**3** Use a clean dish towel to rub the skins off the chillies.

**4** Try not to touch the chillies with your bare hands: use a fork to hold them and slice them open with a sharp knife. Scrape out and discard the seeds, then finely chop the flesh.

**5** Halve the jalapeño chillies, remove their seeds and finely slice them widthways into tiny strips. Mix together both types of chillies, the tomatoes and chopped parsley.

**6** Mix the olive oil, vinegar and a little salt, pour this over the salsa and cover the dish. Chill for up to 3 days.

# Indonesian Satay Sauce

There are many versions of this tasty peanut sauce. This one is very speedy and it tastes delicious drizzled over grilled or barbecued skewers of chicken. For parties, spear chunks of chicken with cocktail sticks and arrange around a bowl of warm sauce.

## Serves 4

INGREDIENTS
200 ml/7 fl oz/scant 1 cup
    coconut cream
60 ml/4 tbsp crunchy peanut butter
5 ml/1 tsp Worcestershire sauce
red Tabasco sauce, to taste
fresh coconut, to garnish (optional)

coconut
cream

*peanut
butter*

Worcestershire
sauce

*red Tabasco
sauce*

*coconut*

## COOK'S TIP

Thick coconut milk can be substituted for coconut cream; coconut milk is usually packed in 400 g/14 oz cans, but take care to buy an unsweetened variety for this recipe.

**1** Pour the coconut cream into a small saucepan and heat it gently over a low heat for about 2 minutes.

**2** Add the peanut butter and stir vigorously until it is blended into the coconut cream. Continue to heat until the mixture is warm but not boiling.

**3** Add the Worcestershire sauce and a dash of Tabasco to taste. Pour into a serving bowl.

**4** Use a potato peeler to shave thin strips from a piece of fresh coconut, if using. Scatter the coconut over the sauce and serve immediately.

# Avocado and Red Pepper Salsa

This simple salsa is a fire-and-ice mixture of hot chilli and cooling avocado. Serve corn chips and crisps for dipping.

## Serves 4

INGREDIENTS
2 ripe avocados
1 red onion
1 red pepper
4 green chillies
30 ml/2 tbsp chopped fresh
   coriander
30 ml/2 tbsp sunflower oil
juice of 1 lemon
salt and pepper

avocados

red onion

red pepper

green chillies

coriander

sunflower oil

lemon juice

## COOK'S TIP

The cut surface of avocados discolour very quickly, so if you plan to prepare this salsa in advance, make sure the avocados are coated with fresh lemon juice to help prevent discoloration.

**1** Halve and stone the avocados. Scoop out and finely dice the flesh. Finely chop the red onion.

**2** Slice the top off the pepper and pull out the central core. Shake out any remaining seeds. Cut the pepper into thin strips and then into dice.

**3** Halve the chillies, remove their seeds and finely chop them. Mix the chillies, coriander, oil, lemon and salt and pepper to taste.

**4** Place the avocado, red onion and pepper in a bowl. Pour in the chilli and coriander dressing and toss the mixture well. Serve immediately.

# Sweet Pepper Salsa

Roasting peppers enhances their flavour and gives them a soft texture – the perfect preparation for salsas. Serve with poached salmon.

## Serves 4

INGREDIENTS
1 red pepper
1 yellow pepper
5 ml/1 tsp cumin seeds
1 red chilli, seeded
30 ml/2 tbsp chopped fresh
  coriander leaves
30 ml/2 tbsp olive oil
15 ml/1 tbsp red wine vinegar
salt and pepper

*yellow pepper*

*red pepper*

*cumin seeds*

*red chilli*

*coriander*

*olive oil*

*red wine vinegar*

**1** Preheat the grill to medium. Place the peppers on a baking sheet and grill them for 8–10 minutes, turning regularly, until their skins have blackened and are blistered.

**2** Place the peppers in a bowl and cover with a clean dish towel. Leave for 5 minutes so the steam helps to lift the skin away from the flesh.

**3** Meanwhile, place the cumin seeds in a small frying pan. Heat gently, stirring, until the seeds start to splutter and release their aroma. Remove the pan from the heat, then tip out the seeds into a mortar and crush them lightly with a pestle.

**4** When the peppers are cool enough to handle, pierce a hole in the bottom of each and squeeze out all of the juices into a bowl.

**5** Peel and core the peppers, discarding the seeds, then process the flesh in a blender or food processor with the chilli and coriander until finely chopped.

**6** Stir in the oil, vinegar and cumin with salt and pepper to taste. Serve at room temperature.

## COOK'S TIP
Choose red, yellow or orange peppers for this salsa as the green variety is less sweet.

# Smoky Tomato Salsa

The smoky flavour in this recipe comes from both the smoked bacon and the commercial liquid smoke marinade. Served with soured cream, this salsa makes a great baked potato filler.

## Serves 4

INGREDIENTS
450 g/1 lb tomatoes
4 rashers smoked streaky bacon
15 ml/1 tbsp vegetable oil
45 ml/3 tbsp chopped fresh
    coriander leaves or parsley
1 garlic clove, finely chopped
15 ml/1 tbsp liquid smoke marinade
juice of 1 lime
salt and pepper

tomatoes

vegetable oil

coriander

smoked streaky bacon

garlic

lime juice

liquid smoke

**1** Skewer the tomatoes on a metal fork and hold them in a gas flame for 1–2 minutes, turning until their skins split and wrinkle. Slip off the skins, halve, scoop out and discard the seeds, then finely dice the tomato flesh.

**2** Cut the bacon into small strips. Heat the oil in a frying pan and cook the bacon for 5 minutes, stirring occasionally, until crisp and browned. Remove from the heat and allow to cool for a few minutes.

**3** Mix the tomatoes, bacon, coriander or parsley, garlic, liquid smoke, lime juice and salt and pepper to taste.

**4** Transfer to a serving bowl and chill until ready to serve.

## VARIATION
Give this smoky salsa an extra kick by adding a dash of Tabasco or a pinch of dried chilli flakes.

# Spicy Avocado Salsa

Avocados discolour quickly so make this sauce just before serving. If you do need to keep it for any length of time, cover closely with clear film and chill in the fridge.

## *Serves 6*

INGREDIENTS
2 large ripe avocados
1 small onion, finely chopped
1 garlic clove, crushed
2 tomatoes
juice of half a lemon
15 ml/1 tbsp olive oil
pinch ground coriander
few drops of Tabasco sauce
salt and pepper
pinch of cayenne pepper

*tomatoes*

*ground coriander*

*olive oil*

*onion*

*Tabasco sauce*

*lemon*

*avocados*

*cayenne pepper*

**1** Halve the avocados, remove the stones and scoop out the flesh into a large bowl.

**2** Using a fork, mash together with the onion and garlic until smooth.

**3** Peel the tomatoes (as for Tomato Salsa), remove the seeds and chop finely. Stir into the avocado mixture with the lemon juice and oil.

**4** Season to taste with coriander, Tabasco sauce, salt and pepper. Spoon into small bowls and sprinkle with cayenne pepper. Serve with corn chips and crisp vegetables or serve as a sauce with chilli and hot tortillas.

# Barbecued Sweetcorn Salsa

Serve this succulent salsa with smoked meats or a juicy grilled gammon steak.

*Serves 4*

INGREDIENTS
2 corn cobs
30 ml/2 tbsp melted butter
4 tomatoes
6 spring onions
1 garlic clove
30 ml/2 tbsp fresh lemon juice
30 ml/2 tbsp olive oil
red Tabasco sauce, to taste
salt and pepper

COOK'S TIP
Make this salsa in summer when fresh cobs of corn are readily available.

*corn cobs*

*butter*

*tomatoes*

*spring onions*

*garlic*

*lemon juice*

*olive oil*

*red Tabasco sauce*

**1** Remove the husks and silky threads covering the corn cobs. Brush the cobs with the melted butter and gently barbecue or grill them for 20–30 minutes, turning occasionally, until tender and tinged brown.

**2** To remove the kernels, stand the cob upright on a chopping board and use a large, heavy knife to slice down the length of the cob.

**3** Skewer the tomatoes in turn on a metal fork and hold in a gas flame for 1–2 minutes, turning until the skin splits and wrinkles. Slip off the skin and dice the tomato flesh.

**4** Finely chop the spring onions and garlic, then mix with the corn and tomato in a small bowl.

**5** Stir the lemon juice and olive oil together, adding Tabasco, salt and pepper to taste.

**6** Pour this over the salsa and stir well. Cover the salsa and leave to infuse at room temperature for 1–2 hours before serving.

# Plantain Salsa

Here is a summery salsa, that is perfect for lazy outdoor eating. Serve with salted potato crisps for dipping.

*Serves 4*

INGREDIENTS
knob of butter
4 ripe plantains
handful of fresh coriander, plus
    extra, to garnish
30 ml/2 tbsp olive oil
5 ml/1 tsp cayenne pepper
salt and pepper

*plantains*

*butter*        *coriander*

*olive oil*

*cayenne
pepper*

**1** Preheat the oven to 200°C/400°F/ Gas 6. Grease four pieces of foil with the knob of butter.

**2** Peel the plantains and place one on each piece of foil. Fold the foil over tightly to form a parcel.

**3** Bake the plantain for 25 minutes, until tender. Alternatively, the plantain may be cooked in the embers of a charcoal barbecue.

**4** Allow the parcels to cool slightly, then remove the plantains, discarding any liquid, and place in a blender or food processor.

**5** Process the plantains with the coriander until fairly smooth. Stir in the olive oil, cayenne pepper and salt and pepper to taste.

**6** Serve immediately as the salsa will discolour and over-thicken if left to cool for too long. Garnish with torn coriander leaves.

## COOK'S TIP
Be sure to choose ripe plantains with blackened skins for this recipe as they will be at their sweetest and tenderest.

# Yellow Tomato and Orange Pepper Salsa

Serve this sunny salsa with spicy sausages or grilled meats.

## Serves 4

INGREDIENTS
4 yellow tomatoes
1 orange pepper
4 spring onions, plus extra, to garnish
handful of fresh coriander leaves
juice of 1 lime
salt and pepper

yellow
tomatoes    orange pepper

spring
onions

coriander

lime juice

**1** Halve the tomatoes. Scoop out the seeds with a teaspoon and discard. Finely chop the flesh.

**2** Spear the pepper on a metal fork and turn it in a gas flame for 1–2 minutes until the skin blisters and chars.

**3** Peel off and discard the skin. Remove the core and scrape out the seeds. Finely chop the flesh.

**4** Finely chop the spring onions and coriander, then mix both with the pepper and tomato flesh.

**5** Squeeze over the lime juice and add salt and pepper to taste. Toss well to mix.

**6** Transfer the salsa to a bowl and chill until ready to serve. Garnish with shreds of spring onion.

## VARIATION
Try using a selection of tomatoes, such as plum or cherry, for a variety of textures and flavours.

# Fresh Tomato and Tarragon Salsa

Plum tomatoes, garlic, olive oil and balsamic vinegar make for a very Mediterranean salsa – try serving this with grilled lamb cutlets or toss it with freshly cooked pasta.

*Serves 4*

INGREDIENTS
8 plum tomatoes
1 small garlic clove
60 ml/4 tbsp olive oil
15 ml/1 tbsp balsamic vinegar
30 ml/2 tbsp chopped fresh
  tarragon, plus extra, to garnish
salt and pepper

*plum
tomatoes*          *garlic*

*olive oil*        *balsamic vinegar*

*tarragon*

## COOK'S TIP
Be sure to serve this salsa at room temperature as the tomatoes taste less sweet, and rather acidic, when chilled.

**1** Skewer the tomatoes in turn on a metal fork and hold in a gas flame for 1–2 minutes, turning until the skin splits and wrinkles.

**2** Slip off the skins and finely chop the tomato flesh.

**3** Using a sharp knife, crush or finely chop the garlic.

**4** Whisk together the olive oil, balsamic vinegar and plenty of salt and pepper.

**5** Finely chop the tarragon and stir it into the olive oil mixture.

**6** Mix the tomatoes and garlic in a bowl and pour the tarragon dressing over. Leave to infuse for at least 1 hour before serving at room temperature. Garnish with shredded tarragon leaves.

# Orange and Chive Salsa

Fresh chives and sweet oranges provide a very cheerful combination of flavours.

## Serves 4

INGREDIENTS
2 large oranges
1 beefsteak tomato
bunch of chives
1 garlic clove
30 ml/2 tbsp olive oil
sea salt

*oranges*

*beefsteak tomato*

*garlic*

*chives*

*olive oil*

**1** Slice the bottom off the orange so that it will stand firmly on a chopping board. Using a large sharp knife, remove the peel by slicing from the top to the bottom of the orange.

**2** Hold the orange in one hand over a bowl. Slice towards the middle of the fruit, to one side of a segment, and then gently twist the knife to ease the segment away from the membrane and out of the orange. Repeat to remove all the segments. Squeeze any juice from the remaining membrane. Prepare the second orange in the same way.

**3** Roughly chop the orange segments and place them in the bowl with the collected juice.

**4** Halve the tomato and use a teaspoon to scoop the seeds into the bowl. Finely dice the flesh and add to the oranges in the bowl.

**5** Hold the bunch of chives neatly together and use a pair of kitchen scissors to snip them into the bowl.

**6** Thinly slice the garlic and stir it into the orange mixture. Pour over the olive oil, season with sea salt and stir well to mix. Serve within 2 hours.

## VARIATION
Add a little diced mozzarella cheese to make a more substantial salsa.

# Aromatic Peach and Cucumber Salsa

Angostura bitters add an unusual and very pleasing flavour to this salsa. Distinctive, sweet-tasting mint complements chicken and other main meat dishes.

*Serves 4*

INGREDIENTS
2 peaches
1 mini cucumber
2.5 ml/½ tsp Angostura bitters
15 ml/1 tbsp olive oil
10 ml/2 tsp fresh lemon juice
30 ml/2 tbsp chopped fresh mint
salt and pepper

*peaches*    *mini cucumber*

*Angostura bitters*    *olive oil*

*lemon juice*    *mint*

## COOK'S TIP
The texture of the peach and the crispness of the cucumber will fade fairly rapidly, so try to prepare this salsa as close to serving time as possible.

**1** Using a small sharp knife, carefully score a line right around the circumference of each peach, cutting just through the skin.

**2** Bring a large pan of water to the boil. Add the peaches and blanch them for 60 seconds. Drain and briefly refresh in cold water.

**3** Peel off and discard the skin. Halve the peaches and remove their stones. Finely dice the flesh and place in a bowl.

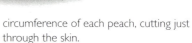

**4** Trim the ends off the cucumber, then finely dice the flesh and stir it into the peaches.

**5** Stir the Angostura bitters, olive oil and lemon juice together and then stir this dressing into the peach mixture.

## VARIATION
Use diced mango in place of peach for an alternative.

**6** Stir in the mint with salt and pepper to taste. Chill and serve within 1 hour.

# Mango and Red Onion Salsa

A very simple salsa, which is livened up by the addition of passion-fruit pulp.

*Serves 4*

INGREDIENTS
1 large ripe mango
1 red onion
2 passion fruit
6 large fresh basil leaves
juice of 1 lime, to taste
sea salt

*mango*     *red onion*

*passion fruit*     *basil*

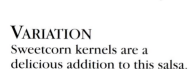

*lime juice*

**1** Holding the mango upright on a chopping board, use a large knife to slice the flesh away from either side of the large flat stone in two portions.

**2** Using a smaller knife, trim away any flesh still clinging to the top and bottom of the stone.

**3** Score the flesh of the mango halves deeply, taking care to avoid cutting through the skin: make parallel incisions about 1 cm/½ in apart; turn and cut lines in the opposite direction. Carefully turn the skin inside out so the flesh stands out like hedgehog spikes. Slice the dice away from the skin.

**4** Finely chop the red onion and place it in a bowl with the mango.

**5** Halve the passion fruit, scoop out the seeds and pulp, and add to the mango mixture.

**6** Tear the basil leaves coarsely and stir them into the salsa with lime juice and a little sea salt to taste. Serve immediately.

## VARIATION
Sweetcorn kernels are a delicious addition to this salsa.

## Quick Barbecue Relish

Making use of storecupboard ingredients, this quick relish is ideal for use with burgers, patties and other quick recipes. It has a slightly tangy flavour.

INGREDIENTS
45 ml/3 tbsp sweet pickle
15 ml/1 tbsp Worcestershire sauce
30 ml/2 tbsp tomato ketchup
10 ml/2 tsp prepared mustard
15 ml/1 tbsp cider vinegar
30 ml/2 tbsp brown sauce

1 Place the pickle in a bowl.

2 Stir in the Worcestershire sauce, tomato ketchup and prepared mustard.

3 Add the vinegar and brown sauce and mix well. Chill and use as required.

## Tomato Relish

A cooked relish which may be served hot or cold. It has a concentrated tomato flavour, making it ideal with pasta, burgers and many of the snack recipes in the book.

INGREDIENTS
15 ml/1 tbsp olive oil
1 onion, chopped
1 garlic clove, crushed
25 g/1 oz/2 tbsp flour
30 ml/2 tbsp tomato ketchup
300 ml/½ pint/1¼ cups passata
5 ml/1 tsp sugar
15 ml/1 tbsp chopped fresh parsley

1 Heat the oil in a pan. Add the onion and garlic clove and sauté for 5 minutes.

2 Add the flour and cook for 1 minute.

3 Stir in the tomato ketchup, passata, sugar and fresh parsley. Bring to the boil. Chill and use as required.

# Chilli Relish

Not for the faint hearted, this is a warm relish ideal with snacks. For a slightly milder flavour, remove the seeds from the chilli before using.

INGREDIENTS
2 large tomatoes
1 red onion
10 ml/2 tsp chilli sauce
15 ml/1 tbsp chopped fresh basil
1 green chilli, chopped
pinch of salt
pinch of sugar

**1** Finely chop the tomatoes and place in a mixing bowl.

**2** Finely chop the onion and add to the tomatoes with the chilli sauce.

**3** Stir in the fresh basil, chilli, salt and sugar. Use as required.

# Cucumber Relish

A cool, refreshing relish, it may also be used as a dip with such recipes as rissoles, or as a topping on burgers and patties. It should be stored for as short a time as possible.

INGREDIENTS
½ cucumber
2 celery sticks, chopped
1 green pepper, seeded and chopped
1 garlic clove, crushed
300 ml/½ pint/1¼ cups natural
    yogurt
15 ml/1 tbsp chopped fresh coriander
freshly ground black pepper

**1** Dice the cucumber and place in a large bowl. Add the celery, green pepper and crushed garlic.

**2** Stir in the yogurt and fresh coriander. Season with the pepper. Cover and chill.

## COOK'S TIP
All these relishes should be used as quickly as possible, but will keep for up to a week in the fridge.

# Bloody Mary Relish

Serve this perfect party salsa with sticks of crunchy cucumber or, on a really special occasion, with freshly shucked oysters.

## Serves 2

INGREDIENTS
4 ripe tomatoes
1 celery stalk
1 garlic clove
2 spring onions
45 ml/3 tbsp tomato juice
Worcestershire sauce, to taste
red Tabasco sauce, to taste
10 ml/2 tsp horseradish sauce
15 ml/1 tbsp vodka
juice of 1 lemon
salt and pepper

1 Halve the tomatoes, celery and garlic. Trim the spring onions.

tomatoes

celery

garlic

spring onions

tomato juice

red Tabasco sauce

vodka

Worcestershire sauce

horseradish sauce

lemon juice

2 Process the vegetables in a blender or food processor until very finely chopped, then transfer them to a bowl.

## VARIATION
Whizz 1–2 fresh seeded, red chillies with the tomatoes instead of adding Tabasco sauce.

3 Stir in the tomato juice and add a few drops of Worcestershire sauce and Tabasco to taste.

4 Stir in the horseradish sauce, vodka and lemon juice. Add salt and freshly ground black pepper, to taste.

# Piquant Pineapple Relish

This fruity sweet-and-sour relish is excellent served with grilled chicken or bacon.

## Serves 4

INGREDIENTS
400 g/14 oz can crushed pineapple
  in natural juice
30 ml/2 tbsp light muscovado sugar
30 ml/2 tbsp wine vinegar
1 garlic clove
4 spring onions
2 red chillies
10 fresh basil leaves
salt and pepper

*pineapple*

*muscovado sugar*

*garlic*

*wine vinegar*

*spring onions*

*red chillies*

*basil*

**1** Drain the pineapple and reserve 60 ml/4 tbsp of the juice.

**2** Place the juice in a small saucepan with the sugar and vinegar, then heat gently, stirring, until the sugar dissolves. Remove from the heat and add salt and pepper to taste.

## VARIATION
This relish tastes extra special when made with fresh pineapple – substitute the juice of a freshly squeezed orange for the canned juice.

**3** Finely chop the garlic and spring onions. Halve the chillies, remove their seeds and finely chop them. Finely shred the basil leaves.

**4** Place the pineapple, garlic, spring onions and chillies in a bowl. Mix well and pour in the sauce. Allow to cool for 5 minutes, then stir in the basil.

# Red Onion Raita

Raita is a traditional Indian accompaniment for hot curries. It is also delicious served with poppadoms as a dip.

*Serves 4*

INGREDIENTS
5 ml/1 tsp cumin seeds
1 small garlic clove
1 small green chilli, seeded
1 large red onion
150 ml/¼ pint/⅔ cup natural
    yogurt
30 ml/2 tbsp chopped fresh
    coriander, plus extra, to garnish
2.5 ml/½ tsp sugar
salt

*cumin*      *garlic*      *green chilli*

*red onion*      *coriander*

*yogurt*      *sugar*

## COOK'S TIP

For an extra tangy raita stir in 15 ml/1 tbsp lemon juice. To make a pretty garnish, reserve a few thin wedges of onion, before chopping the rest.

**1** Heat a small pan and dry-fry the cumin seeds for 1–2 minutes, until they release their aroma and begin to pop.

**2** Lightly crush the seeds in a pestle and mortar or flatten them with the heel of a heavy-bladed knife.

**3** Finely chop the garlic, chilli and red onion. Stir into the yogurt with the crushed cumin seeds and coriander.

**4** Add sugar and salt to taste. Spoon the raita into a small bowl and chill until ready to serve. Garnish with extra coriander before serving.

# Spicy Sweetcorn Relish

Serve this simple spicy relish with Red Onion Raita, Sweet Mango Relish and a plateful of crisp onion bhajis for a fabulous Indian-style starter.

## *Serves 4*

INGREDIENTS
1 large onion
1 red chilli, seeded
2 garlic cloves
30 ml/2 tbsp vegetable oil
5 ml/1 tsp black mustard seeds
10 ml/2 tsp hot curry powder
320 g/11¼ oz can sweetcorn
grated rind and juice of 1 lime
45 ml/3 tbsp chopped fresh
   coriander
salt and pepper

onion   red
         chilli   garlic

vegetable oil   mustard
                 seeds   curry powder

lime
juice
and rind   sweetcorn

coriander

### COOK'S TIP
Opt for canned rather than frozen sweetcorn if possible as the kernels are plump, moist and ready to eat.

**1** Chop the onion, chilli and garlic. Heat the oil in a large frying pan and cook the onion, chilli and garlic over a high heat for 5 minutes, until the onions are just beginning to brown.

**2** Stir in the mustard seeds and curry powder, then cook for a further 2 minutes, stirring, until the seeds start to splutter and the onions are browned.

**3** Remove the fried onion mixture from the heat and allow to cool. Place in a glass bowl. Drain the sweetcorn and stir into the onion mixture.

**4** Add the lime rind and juice, coriander and salt and pepper to taste. Cover and serve at room temperature.

# Toffee Onion Relish

Slow, gentle cooking reduces the onions to a soft, caramelised relish in this recipe.

*Serves 4*

INGREDIENTS
3 large onions
50 g/2 oz/4 tbsp butter
30 ml/2 tbsp olive oil
30 ml/2 tbsp light muscovado sugar
30 ml/2 tbsp pickled capers
30 ml/2 tbsp chopped fresh parsley
salt and pepper

*onions*

*olive oil*

*muscovado sugar*

*butter*

*capers*

*parsley*

**1** Peel the onions and halve them vertically, through the core, then slice them thinly.

**2** Heat the butter and oil together in a large saucepan. Add the onions and sugar and cook very gently for 30 minutes over a low heat, stirring occasionally, until reduced to a soft rich brown toffeed mixture.

**3** Roughly chop the capers and stir into the toffee onions. Allow to cool completely.

**4** Stir in the chopped parsley and add salt and pepper to taste. Cover and chill until ready to serve.

## VARIATION
Try making this recipe with red onions or shallots for a subtle variation in flavour.

# Tart Tomato Relish

The whole lime used in this recipe adds a
pleasantly sour after-taste. Serve with grilled or
roast pork or lamb.

## Serves 4

INGREDIENTS
2 pieces stem ginger
1 lime
450 g/1 lb cherry tomatoes
115 g/4 oz/½ cup dark muscovado
   sugar
100 ml/3½ fl oz/scant ½ cup white
   wine vinegar
5 ml/1 tsp salt

stem
ginger

cherry
tomatoes

muscovado
sugar

white wine
vinegar

lime

**1** Coarsely chop the ginger. Slice the
whole lime thinly, then chop it into small
pieces; do not remove the rind.

**2** Place the whole tomatoes, sugar,
vinegar, salt, ginger and lime together
in a saucepan.

**3** Bring to the boil, stirring until the
sugar dissolves, then simmer rapidly for
45 minutes. Stir regularly until the liquid
has evaporated and the relish is
thickened and pulpy.

**4** Allow the relish to cool for about
5 minutes, then spoon it into clean jars.
Cool completely, cover and store in the
fridge for up to 1 month.

## VARIATION
If preferred, use ordinary
tomatoes, roughly chopped, in
place of the cherry tomatoes.

# Chilli Relish

This spicy relish will keep for at least a week in the fridge. Serve it with bangers and burgers.

## *Serves 8*

INGREDIENTS
6 tomatoes
1 onion
1 red pepper, seeded
2 garlic cloves
30 ml/2 tbsp olive oil
5 ml/1 tsp ground cinnamon
5 ml/1 tsp chilli flakes
5 ml/1 tsp ground ginger
5 ml/1 tsp salt
2.5 ml/½ tsp freshly ground
  black pepper
75 g/3 oz/⅓ cup light muscovado
  sugar
75 ml/5 tbsp cider vinegar
handful of fresh basil leaves

*tomatoes*   *onion*
*red pepper*   *olive oil*
*garlic*
*ground cinnamon*   *chilli flakes*
*ground ginger*
*muscovado sugar*
*cider vinegar*   *basil*

COOK'S TIP
This relish thickens slightly on cooling so do not worry if the mixture seems a little wet at the end of step 5.

**1** Skewer each of the tomatoes in turn on a metal fork and hold in a gas flame for 1–2 minutes, turning until the skin splits and wrinkles. Slip off the skins, then roughly chop the tomatoes.

**2** Roughly chop the onion, red pepper and garlic. Heat the oil in a saucepan. Add the onion, red pepper and garlic to the pan.

**3** Cook gently for 5–8 minutes, until the pepper is softened. Add the chopped tomatoes, cover and cook for 5 minutes, until the tomatoes release their juices.

**4** Stir in the cinnamon, chilli flakes, ginger, salt, pepper, sugar and vinegar. Bring gently to the boil, stirring until the sugar dissolves.

**5** Simmer, uncovered, for 20 minutes, until the mixture is pulpy. Stir in the basil leaves and check the seasoning.

**6** Allow to cool completely then transfer to a glass jar or a plastic container with a tightly fitting lid. Store, covered, in the fridge.

# Sweet Mango Relish

Stir a spoonful of this relish into soups and stews for added flavour or serve it with a wedge of Cheddar cheese and chunks of crusty bread.

### VARIATION
Select alternative spices to suit your own taste: for example, add juniper berries in place of the star anise or try cumin seeds.

## Makes 750 ml/1¼ pints/ 3 cups

INGREDIENTS
2 large mangoes
1 cooking apple
2 shallots
4 cm/1½ in piece root ginger
2 garlic cloves
115 g/4 oz/cup small sultanas
2 star anise
5 ml/1 tsp ground cinnamon
2.5 ml/½ tsp dried chilli flakes
2.5 ml/½ tsp salt
175 ml/6 fl oz/¾ cup cider vinegar
130 g/3½ oz/scant ½ cup light
   muscovado sugar

*mangoes*

*shallots*

*root ginger*

*cooking apple*

*garlic*

*sultanas*

*star anise*

*ground cinnamon*

*chilli flakes*

*cider vinegar*

*muscovado sugar*

**1** Hold the mangoes, one at a time, upright on a chopping board and use a large knife to slice the flesh away from either side of the large flat stone in two portions. Using a smaller knife, carefully trim away any flesh still clinging to the top and bottom of the stone.

**2** Score the flesh of the mango halves deeply, taking care to avoid cutting through the skin: make parallel incisions about 1 cm/½ in apart; turn and cut lines in the opposite direction. Carefully turn the skin inside out so the flesh stands out like hedgehog spikes. Slice the dice away from the skin.

**3** Using a sharp knife, peel and roughly chop the apple, shallots, ginger and garlic.

**4** Place the mango, apple, shallots, ginger, garlic and sultanas in a large pan. Add the spices, salt, vinegar and sugar.

**5** Bring to the boil, stirring until the sugar dissolves. Reduce the heat and simmer gently for 45 minutes, stirring occasionally, until the chutney has reduced and thickened.

**6** Allow the chutney to cool for about 5 minutes, then pot it into clean jars. Cool completely, cover and store in the fridge for up to 2 months.

## Mayonnaise

Mayonnaise is a simple emulsion made with egg yolks and oil. For consistent results, ensure that both egg yolks and oil are at room temperature before combining – around 21°C/70°F. Home-made mayonnaise is made with raw egg yolks and may therefore be considered unsuitable for young children, pregnant mothers and the elderly.

*Makes about 300 ml/12 fl oz/1½ cups*

INGREDIENTS
2 egg yolks
5 ml/1 tsp French mustard
150 ml/5 fl oz/⅔ cup extra-virgin olive oil, French or Italian
150 ml/5 fl oz/⅔ cup groundnut or sunflower oil
10 ml/2 tsp white wine vinegar
salt and pepper

**2** Add the olive oil a little at a time while the processor is running. When the mixture is thick, add the remainder of the oil in a slow steady stream.

**1** Place the egg yolks and mustard in a food processor and blend smoothly.

**3** Add the vinegar and season to taste with salt and pepper.

### COOK'S TIP

Should mayonnaise separate during blending, add 30 ml/2 tbsp boiling water and beat until smooth. Store mayonnaise in the refrigerator for up to 1 week, sealed in a screw-top jar.

## Blue Cheese and Chive Dressing

Blue cheese dressings have a strong robust flavour and are well suited to winter salad leaves: escarole, chicory and radicchio.

*Makes about 350 ml/14 fl oz/1¾ cups*

INGREDIENTS
75 g/3 oz blue cheese, Stilton, Bleu d'Auvergne or Gorgonzola
150 ml/5 fl oz/⅔ cup medium-fat plain yogurt
45 ml/3 tbsp olive oil, preferably Italian
30 ml/2 tbsp lemon juice
15 ml/1 tbsp chopped fresh chives
black pepper

**2** Add the remainder of the yogurt, the olive oil and lemon juice.

**1** Remove the rind from the cheese. Place the cheese with a third of the yogurt in a mixing bowl and combine smoothly with a wooden spoon.

**3** Stir in the chives and season to taste with freshly ground black pepper.

# French Dressing

French vinaigrette is the most widely used salad dressing and is appreciated for its simplicity and style. For the best flavour, use the finest extra-virgin olive oil and go easy on the vinegar.

*Makes about 125 ml/4 fl oz/¹/₂ cup*

INGREDIENTS
90 ml/6 tbsp/¹/₃ cup extra-virgin olive
   oil, French or Italian
15 ml/1 tbsp white wine vinegar
5 ml/1 tsp French mustard
pinch of caster (superfine) sugar

**2** Add the mustard and sugar.

**1** Place the olive oil and vinegar in a screw-top jar.

**3** Replace the lid and shake well.

## COOK'S TIP
Liquid dressings that contain extra-virgin olive oil should be stored at room temperature. Refrigeration can cause them to solidify.

# French Herb Dressing

The delicate scents of fresh herbs combine especially well in a French dressing. Toss with a simple green salad and serve with good cheese and wine.

*Makes about 125 ml/4 fl oz/¹/₂ cup*

INGREDIENTS
60 ml/4 tbsp extra-virgin olive oil,
   French or Italian
30 ml/2 tbsp groundnut or sunflower
   oil
15 ml/1 tbsp lemon juice
60 ml/4 tbsp finely chopped fresh
   herbs: parsley, chives, tarragon and
   marjoram
pinch of caster (superfine) sugar

**2** Add the lemon juice, herbs and sugar.

**1** Place the olive and groundnut oil in a screw-top jar.

**3** Replace the lid and shake well.

# Thai Red Curry Sauce

Serve this with mini spring rolls or spicy Indonesian crackers, or toss it into freshly cooked rice noodles for a delicious main-meal accompaniment.

## *Serves 4*

INGREDIENTS

200 ml/7 fl oz/scant 1 cup coconut
   cream
10–15 ml/2–3 tsp Thai red curry paste
4 spring onions, plus extra, to garnish
30 ml/2 tbsp chopped fresh
   coriander
1 red chilli, seeded and thinly sliced
   into rings
5 ml/1 tsp soy sauce
juice of 1 lime
sugar, to taste
25 g/1 oz/¼ cup dry-roasted
   peanuts
salt and pepper

coconut cream

Thai red curry paste

spring onions

soy sauce

red chilli

coriander

lime juice

sugar

dry-roasted peanuts

**1** Pour the coconut cream into a small bowl and stir in the curry paste.

**2** Trim and finely slice the spring onions diagonally. Stir into the coconut cream with the coriander and chilli.

## COOK'S TIP
The dip may be prepared in advance up to the end of step 3. Sprinkle the peanuts over just before serving.

**3** Stir in the soy sauce, lime juice, sugar, salt and pepper to taste. Pour the sauce into a small serving bowl.

**4** Finely chop the dry-roasted peanuts and sprinkle them over the sauce. Serve immediately. Garnish with spring onions sliced lengthways.

# Melting Cheese Dip

This is a classic fondue in true Swiss style. It should be served with cubes of crusty, day-old bread, but it is also good with chunks of spicy, cured sausage such as chorizo.

## Serves 2

INGREDIENTS
1 garlic clove, finely chopped
150 ml/¼ pint/⅔ cup dry white wine
150 g/5 oz Gruyère cheese
5 ml/1 tsp cornflour
15 ml/1 tbsp Kirsch
salt and pepper

*garlic*  *white wine*

*Gruyère cheese*  *cornflour*

*Kirsch*

**1** Place the garlic and wine in a small saucepan and bring gently to the boil. Simmer for 3–4 minutes.

**2** Coarsely grate the cheese and stir it into the wine. Continue to stir as the cheese melts.

**3** Blend the cornflour to a smooth paste with the Kirsch and pour into the pan, stirring. Bring to the boil, stirring continuously, until the sauce is smooth and thickened.

**4** Add salt and pepper to taste. Serve immediately or, better still, transfer to a fondue pan and place over a spirit burner to keep it hot. Garnish with black pepper.

## COOK'S TIP
Gruyère is a tasty cheese that melts incredibly well. Don't substitute other cheeses.

# Hummus

This nutritious dip can be served with vegetable crudités or packed into salad-filled pitta, but it is best spread thickly on hot buttered toast.

*Serves 4*

INGREDIENTS

400 g/14 oz can chick-peas,
   drained
2 garlic cloves
30 ml/2 tbsp tahini or smooth
   peanut butter
60 ml/4 tbsp olive oil
juice of 1 lemon
2.5 ml/½ tsp cayenne pepper
15 ml/1 tbsp sesame seeds
sea salt

garlic

sea salt

chick-peas

olive oil

tahini

lemon juice

cayenne pepper

sesame seeds

## COOK'S TIP

Tahini is a thick smooth and oily paste made from sesame seeds. It is available from health-food shops and large supermarkets. Tahini is a classic ingredient in hummus, this Middle-Eastern dip; peanut butter would not be used in a traditional recipe but it is a useful substitute.

**1** Rinse the chick-peas well and place in a blender or food processor with the garlic and a good pinch of sea salt. Process until very finely chopped.

**2** Add the tahini or peanut butter and process until fairly smooth. With the motor still running, slowly pour in the oil and lemon juice.

**3** Stir in the cayenne pepper and add more salt, to taste. If the mixture is too thick, stir in a little cold water. Transfer the purée to a serving bowl.

**4** Heat a small non-stick pan and add the sesame seeds. Cook for 2–3 minutes, shaking the pan, until the seeds are golden. Allow to cool, then sprinkle over the purée.

# Cannellini Bean Dip

This soft bean dip or pâté is good spread on wheaten crackers or toasted muffins. Alternatively, it can be served with wedges of tomato and a crisp green salad.

## Serves 4

INGREDIENTS
400 g/14 oz can cannellini beans
grated rind and juice of 1 lemon
30 ml/2 tbsp olive oil
1 garlic clove, finely chopped
30 ml/2 tbsp chopped fresh parsley
red Tabasco sauce, to taste
cayenne pepper
salt and pepper

cannellini beans

olive oil

lemon juice and rind

garlic

parsley

red Tabasco sauce

cayenne pepper

## VARIATION
Other beans can be used for this dip, for example butter beans or kidney beans.

1 Drain the beans in a sieve and rinse them well under cold water. Transfer to a shallow bowl.

2 Use a potato masher to roughly purée the beans, then stir in the lemon juice and olive oil.

3 Stir in the chopped garlic and parsley. Add Tabasco sauce and salt and pepper to taste.

4 Spoon the mixture into a small bowl and dust lightly with cayenne pepper. Chill until ready to serve.

143

# Chilli Bean Dip

This creamy bean dip is best served warm with triangles of grilled pitta bread or a bowl of crunchy tortilla chips.

## Serves 4

INGREDIENTS
2 garlic cloves
1 onion
2 green chillies
30 ml/2 tbsp vegetable oil
5–10 ml/1–2 tsp hot chilli powder
400 g/14 oz can kidney beans
75 g/3 oz mature Cheddar
  cheese, grated
1 red chilli, seeded
salt and pepper

garlic

green chillies

onion

vegetable oil

chilli powder

kidney beans

Cheddar cheese

red chilli

**1** Finely chop the garlic and onion. Seed and finely chop the green chillies.

**2** Heat the oil in a large sauté pan or deep frying pan and add the garlic, onion, green chillies and chilli powder. Cook gently for 5 minutes, stirring regularly, until the onions are softened and transparent, but not browned.

**3** Drain the kidney beans, reserving the liquor. Blend all but 30 ml/2 tbsp of the beans to a purée in a food processor.

**4** Add the puréed beans to the pan with 30–45 ml/2–3 tbsp of the reserved liquor. Heat gently, stirring to mix well.

**5** Stir in the whole beans and the Cheddar cheese. Cook gently for about 2–3 minutes, stirring until the cheese melts. Add salt and pepper to taste.

**6** Cut the red chilli into tiny strips. Spoon the dip into four individual serving bowls and scatter the chilli strips over the top. Serve warm.

## COOK'S TIP

For a dip with a coarser texture, do not purée the beans, instead mash them with a potato masher.

# Lemon and Coconut Dhal

A warm spicy dish, this can be served either as a dip with poppadoms or as a main-meal accompaniment.

### VARIATION
Try making this dhal with yellow split peas: they take longer to cook and a little extra water has to be added but the result is equally tasty.

## Serves 8

INGREDIENTS
5 cm/2 in piece root ginger
1 onion
2 garlic cloves
2 small red chillies, seeded
30 ml/2 tbsp sunflower oil
5 ml/1 tsp cumin seeds
150 g/5 oz/⅔ cup red lentils
250 ml/8 fl oz/1 cup water
15 ml/1 tbsp hot curry paste
200 ml/7 fl oz/scant 1 cup
  coconut cream
juice of 1 lemon
handful of fresh coriander leaves
25 g/1 oz/¼ cup flaked almonds
salt and pepper

root ginger   onion   garlic

cumin seeds   sunflower oil   red chillies

red lentils

curry paste

coconut cream   lemon juice

coriander   flaked almonds

**1** Use a vegetable peeler to peel the ginger and finely chop it with the onion, garlic and chillies.

**2** Heat the oil in a large shallow saucepan. Add the ginger, onion, garlic, chillies and cumin. Cook for 5 minutes, until softened but not coloured.

**3** Stir the lentils, water and curry paste into the pan. Bring to the boil, cover and cook gently over a low heat for 15–20 minutes, stirring occasionally, until the lentils are just tender and not yet broken.

**4** Stir in all but 30 ml/2 tbsp of the coconut cream. Bring to the boil and cook, uncovered, for a further 15–20 minutes, until the mixture is thick and pulpy. Remove from the heat, then stir in the lemon juice and the whole coriander leaves. Add salt and pepper to taste.

**5** Heat a large frying pan and cook the flaked almonds for one or two minutes on each side until golden brown. Stir about three-quarters of the toasted almonds into the dhal.

**6** Transfer the dhal to a serving bowl and swirl in the remaining coconut cream. Scatter the reserved almonds on top and serve warm.

# Butternut Squash and Parmesan Dip

Butternut squash has a rich, nutty flavour and tastes especially good roasted. Serve this dip with melba toast or cheese straws.

## Serves 4

INGREDIENTS
1 butternut squash
15 g/½ oz/1 tbsp butter
4 garlic cloves, unpeeled
30 ml/2 tbsp freshly grated
  Parmesan cheese
45–75 ml/3–5 tbsp double cream
salt and pepper

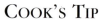

*butternut squash*

*garlic*

*butter*

*Parmesan cheese*

*double cream*

## COOK'S TIP

If you don't have a blender or food processor, simply mash the squash in a bowl using a potato masher, then beat in the grated cheese and cream using a wooden spoon.

**1** Preheat the oven to 200°C/400°F/Gas 6. Halve the butternut squash lengthways, then scoop out and discard the seeds.

**3** Arrange both halves in a small roasting tin and dot them with the butter. Sprinkle with salt and pepper and roast for 20 minutes.

**2** Use a small, sharp knife to deeply score the flesh in a criss-cross pattern: cut as close to the skin as possible, but take care not to cut through it.

**4** Tuck the unpeeled garlic cloves around the squash in the roasting tin and continue baking for 20 minutes, until the butternut squash is tender and softened.

**5** Scoop the flesh out of the squash shells and place it in a blender or food processor. Slip the garlic cloves out of their skins and add to the squash. Process until smooth.

## VARIATION

Try making this dip with
pumpkin or other types of
squash, such as acorn squash or
New Zealand kabocha.

**6** With the motor running, add all but
15 ml/1 tsp of the Parmesan cheese and
then the cream. Check the seasoning
and spoon the dip into a serving bowl: it
is at its best served warm. Scatter the
reserved cheese over the dip.

# Blue Cheese Dip

This dip can be mixed up in next-to-no-time and is delicious served with pears. Add more yogurt to make a great dressing.

## Serves 4

INGREDIENTS
150 g/5 oz blue cheese, such as
   Stilton or Danish Blue
150 g/5oz/⅔ cup soft cheese
75 ml/5 tbsp Greek-style yogurt
salt and pepper

*blue
cheese*

*soft
cheese*

*Greek-style
yogurt*

**1** Crumble the blue cheese into a bowl. Using a wooden spoon, beat the cheese to soften it.

**2** Add the soft cheese and beat well to blend the two cheeses together.

**3** Gradually beat in the Greek-style yogurt, adding enough to give you the consistency you prefer.

**4** Season with lots of black pepper and a little salt. Chill until ready to serve.

## COOK'S TIP

This is a very thick dip to which you can add a little more Greek-style yogurt, or stir in a little milk, for a softer consistency.

# Saucy Tomato Dip

This versatile dip is delicious served with absolutely anything and can be made up to 24 hours in advance.

*Serves 4*

INGREDIENTS
1 shallot
2 garlic cloves
handful of fresh basil leaves, plus
  extra, to garnish
500 g/1¼ lb ripe tomatoes
30 ml/2 tbsp olive oil
2 green chillies
salt and pepper

*shallot*

*garlic*

*basil*

*tomatoes*

*green chillies*

*olive oil*

**1** Peel and halve the shallot and garlic cloves. Place in a blender or food processor with the basil leaves, then process the ingredients until they are very finely chopped.

**2** Halve the tomatoes and add to the shallot mixture. Pulse the power until the mixture is well blended and the tomatoes are finely chopped.

**3** With the motor still running, slowly pour in the olive oil. Add salt and pepper to taste.

**4** Halve the chillies lengthways and remove their seeds. Finely slice them across into tiny strips and stir them into the tomato mixture. Serve at room temperature. Garnish with a few torn basil leaves.

## COOK'S TIP
This dip is best made with full-flavoured sun-ripened tomatoes. In winter, use a drained 400 g/14 oz can of plum tomatoes.

# Mellow Garlic Dip

Two whole heads of garlic may seem like a lot but, once cooked, it becomes sweet and mellow. Serve with crunchy bread sticks and crisps.

## Serves 4

INGREDIENTS
2 whole garlic heads
15 ml/1 tbsp olive oil
60 ml/4 tbsp mayonnaise
75 ml/5 tbsp Greek-style yogurt
5 ml/1 tsp wholegrain mustard
salt and pepper

*garlic*

*olive oil*

*mayonnaise*

*Greek-style
yogurt*

*wholegrain
mustard*

**1** Preheat the oven to 200°C/400°F/ Gas 6. Separate the garlic cloves and place them in a small roasting tin.

**3** Trim off the root end of each roasted garlic clove. Peel the cloves and discard the skins.

**2** Pour the olive oil over the garlic cloves and turn them with a spoon to coat them evenly. Roast for 20–30 minutes, until the garlic is tender and softened. Leave to cool for 5 minutes.

**4** Place the roasted garlic on a chopping board and sprinkle with salt. Mash with a fork until puréed.

**5** Place the garlic in a small bowl and stir in the mayonnaise, yogurt and wholegrain mustard.

## COOK'S TIP

If you are already cooking on a barbecue, leave the garlic heads whole and cook them on the hot barbecue until tender, then peel and mash.

## VARIATION

For a low fat version of this dip, use reduced-fat mayonnaise and low fat natural yogurt.

**6** Check and adjust the seasoning, then spoon the dip into a bowl. Cover and chill until ready to serve.

# Tzatziki

Serve this classic Greek dip with strips of toasted pitta bread.

*Serves 4*

INGREDIENTS
1 mini cucumber
4 spring onions
1 garlic clove
200 ml/7 fl oz/scant 1 cup Greek-style yogurt
45 ml/3 tbsp chopped fresh mint
fresh mint sprig, to garnish (optional)
salt and pepper

*mini cucumber*

*spring onions*

*garlic*

*Greek-style yogurt*

*mint*

## COOK'S TIP

Choose Greek-style yogurt for this dip – it has a higher fat content than most yogurts, which gives it a deliciously rich, creamy texture.

**1** Trim the ends from the cucumber, then cut it into 5 mm/¼ in dice.

**2** Trim the spring onions and garlic, then chop both very finely.

**3** Beat the yogurt until smooth, if necessary, then gently stir in the cucumber, onions, garlic and mint.

**4** Transfer the mixture to a serving bowl and add salt and plenty of freshly ground black pepper to taste. Chill until ready to serve and then garnish with a small mint sprig, if you like.

# Soured Cream Cooler

This cooling dip is a perfect accompaniment to hot and spicy Mexican dishes. Alternatively, serve it as a snack with the fieriest tortilla chips you can find.

*Serves 2*

INGREDIENTS

1 small yellow pepper
2 small tomatoes
30 ml/2 tbsp chopped fresh parsley
150 ml/¼ pint/⅔ cup soured cream
grated lemon rind, to garnish

*yellow pepper*      *tomatoes*

*parsley*      *soured cream*

*lemon rind*

## VARIATION
Use finely diced avocado or cucumber in place of the pepper or tomato.

**1** Halve the pepper lengthways. Remove the core and seeds, then cut the flesh into tiny dice.

**2** Halve the tomatoes, then scoop out and discard the seeds and cut the flesh into tiny dice.

**3** Stir the pepper and tomato dice and the chopped parsley into the soured cream and mix well.

**4** Spoon the dip into a small bowl and chill. Garnish with grated lemon rind before serving.

# Creamy Aubergine Dip

Spread this velvet-textured dip thickly on to toasted rounds of bread, then top them with slivers of sun-dried tomato to make wonderful, Italian-style crostini.

*Serves 4*

INGREDIENTS
1 large aubergine
1 small onion
2 garlic cloves
30 ml/2 tbsp olive oil
60 ml/4 tbsp chopped fresh parsley
75 ml/5 tbsp crème fraîche
red Tabasco sauce, to taste
juice of 1 lemon, to taste
salt and pepper

aubergine

garlic

onion

olive oil

parsley

crème fraîche

red Tabasco sauce

lemon juice

**1** Preheat the grill to medium. Place the whole aubergine on a baking sheet and grill it for 20–30 minutes, turning occasionally, until the skin is blackened and wrinkled, and the aubergine feels soft when squeezed.

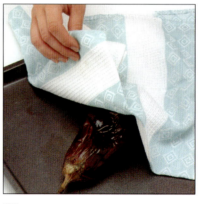

**2** Cover the aubergine with a clean dish towel and leave it to cool for about 5 minutes.

**3** Finely chop the onion and garlic. Heat the oil in a frying pan and cook the onion and garlic for 5 minutes, until softened, but not browned.

**4** Peel the skin from the aubergine. Mash the flesh with a large fork or potato masher to make a pulpy purée.

**5** Stir in the onion and garlic, parsley and crème fraîche. Add Tabasco, lemon juice and salt and pepper to taste.

**6** Transfer the dip to a serving bowl and serve warm or leave to cool and serve at room temperature.

## COOK'S TIP
The aubergine can be roasted in the oven at 200°C/400°F/Gas 6 for 20 minutes, if preferred.

# Thousand Island Dip

This variation on the classic Thousand Island dressing is far removed from the original version, but can be served in the same way – with grilled king prawns laced on to bamboo skewers for dipping or with a simple mixed seafood salad.

## Serves 4

INGREDIENTS
4 sun-dried tomatoes in oil
4 tomatoes
150 g/5 oz/⅔ cup soft cheese
60 ml/4 tbsp mayonnaise
30 ml/2 tbsp tomato purée
30 ml/2 tbsp chopped fresh parsley
grated rind and juice of 1 lemon
red Tabasco sauce, to taste
5 ml/1 tsp Worcestershire or soy sauce
salt and pepper

sun-dried tomatoes in oil

soft cheese

tomatoes

parsley

mayonnaise

tomato purée

Worcestershire sauce

red Tabasco sauce

lemon juice and rind

**1** Drain the sun-dried tomatoes on kitchen paper to remove excess oil, then finely chop them.

**2** Skewer each tomato in turn on a metal fork and hold in a gas flame for 1–2 minutes, until the skin wrinkles and splits. Slip off and discard the skins, then halve the tomatoes and scoop out the seeds with a teaspoon. Finely chop the tomato flesh.

**3** Beat the soft cheese, then gradually beat in the mayonnaise and tomato purée.

**4** Stir in the chopped parsley and sun-dried tomatoes, then add the chopped tomatoes and their seeds and mix well.

**5** Add the lemon rind and juice and Tabasco to taste. Stir in Worcestershire or soy sauce, and salt and pepper.

**6** Transfer the dip to a bowl, cover and chill until ready to serve.

# Fat-free Saffron Dip

Serve this mild dip with fresh vegetable crudités - it is particularly good with florets of cauliflower.

*Serves 4*

INGREDIENTS
15 ml/1 tbsp boiling water
small pinch of saffron strands
200 g/7 oz/scant 1 cup fat-free
    fromage frais
10 fresh chives
10 fresh basil leaves
salt and pepper

*saffron strands*

*fromage frais*

*chives*

*basil leaves*

**1** Pour the boiling water into a small container and add the saffron strands. Leave to infuse for 3 minutes.

**2** Beat the fromage frais until smooth, then stir in the infused saffron liquid.

**3** Use a pair of scissors to snip the chives into the dip. Tear the basil leaves into small pieces and stir them in.

**4** Add salt and pepper to taste. Serve immediately.

## VARIATION
Leave out the saffron and add a squeeze of lemon or lime juice instead.

# Spiced Carrot Dip

This is a delicious low-fat dip with a sweet and spicy flavour. Serve wheat crackers or fiery tortilla chips as accompaniments for dipping.

## Serves 4

INGREDIENTS
1 onion
3 carrots, plus extra, to garnish
grated rind and juice of 2 oranges
15 ml/1 tbsp hot curry paste
150 ml/¼ pint/⅔ cup low-fat
   natural yogurt
handful of fresh basil leaves
15–30 ml/1–2 tbsp fresh lemon
   juice, to taste
red Tabasco sauce, to taste
salt and pepper

*onion*

*carrots*

*orange rind and juice*

*curry paste*

*basil*

*lemon juice*

*low fat natural yogurt*

*red Tabasco sauce*

## VARIATION
Greek-style yogurt or soured cream may be used in place of the natural yogurt to make a richer, creamy dip.

**1** Finely chop the onion. Peel and grate the carrots. Place the onion, carrots, orange rind and juice and curry paste in a small saucepan. Bring to the boil, cover and simmer for 10 minutes, until tender.

**2** Process the mixture in a blender or food processor until smooth. Leave to cool completely.

**3** Stir in the yogurt, then tear the basil leaves into small pieces and stir them into the carrot mixture.

**4** Add the lemon juice, Tabasco, salt and pepper to taste. Serve within a few hours at room temperature. Garnish with grated carrot.

# Basil and Lemon Mayonnaise

This dip is based on fresh mayonnaise flavoured with lemon juice and two types of basil. Serve with salads, baked potatoes or as a delicious dip for French fries.

## Serves 4

INGREDIENTS
2 size 1 egg yolks
15 ml/1 tbsp lemon juice
150 ml/¼ pint/⅔ cup olive oil
150 ml/¼ pint/⅔ cup sunflower oil
4 garlic cloves
handful of green basil leaves
handful of opal basil leaves
salt and pepper

*egg yolks*

*garlic*

*lemon juice*

*olive oil*

*sunflower oil*

*green basil*

*opal basil*

**1** Place the egg yolks and lemon juice in a blender or food processor and process them briefly until lightly blended.

**2** In a jug, stir together both oils. With the machine running, pour in the oil very slowly, a little at a time.

**3** Once half of the oil has been added, the remaining oil can be incorporated more quickly. Continue processing to form a thick, creamy mayonnaise.

**4** Peel and crush the garlic cloves. Alternatively, place them on a chopping board and sprinkle with salt, then flatten them with the heel of a heavy-bladed knife and chop the flesh. Flatten the garlic again to make a coarse purée.

**5** Tear both types of basil into small pieces and stir into the mayonnaise with the crushed garlic.

**6** Add salt and pepper to taste, then transfer the dip to a serving dish. Cover and chill until ready to serve.

## COOK'S TIP
Make sure all the ingredients are at room temperature before you start to help prevent the mixture from curdling.

# Curry Mayonnaise with Prawn and Tomato Salad

Curry spices add an unexpected twist to this dressing. Warm flavours combine especially well with sweet prawns and grated apple.

## Serves 4

**INGREDIENTS**
1 ripe tomato
½ iceberg lettuce, shredded
1 small onion
1 small bunch fresh coriander
15 ml/1 tbsp lemon juice
salt
450 g/1 lb cooked peeled prawns (shrimp)
1 apple, peeled

**DRESSING**
75 ml/5 tbsp mayonnaise
5 ml/1 tsp mild curry paste
15 ml/1 tbsp tomato ketchup

**TO DECORATE**
8 whole prawns
8 lemon wedges
4 sprigs fresh coriander

**2** Finely shred the lettuce, onion and coriander. Add the tomato, moisten with lemon juice and season with salt.

**3** To make the dressing, combine the mayonnaise, curry paste and tomato ketchup in a small bowl. Add 30 ml/2 tbsp water to thin the dressing and season to taste with salt.

**1** To peel the tomato, pierce the skin with a knife and immerse in boiling water for 20 seconds. Drain and cool under running water. Peel off the skin. Halve the tomato, push the seeds out with your thumb and discard them. Cut the flesh into large dice.

*prawns (shrimp)*    *coriander*    *tomato*    *apple*    *lemon*    *onion*

**4** Combine the prawns (shrimp) with the dressing. Quarter and core the apple and grate into the mixture.

## COOK'S TIP

Fresh coriander is inclined to wilt if kept out of water. Keep it in a jar of water in the refrigerator covered with a plastic bag and it will stay fresh for several days.

**5** Distribute the shredded lettuce mixture between 4 plates or bowls. Pile the prawn mixture in the centre of each and decorate with 2 whole prawns, 2 lemon wedges and a sprig of coriander.

# Fresh Mango Dressing with Grilled Fish

Combining the flavours of mango with hot chili, ginger and lime, this rich, tangy dressing is perfect for outdoor summer meals.

*Serves 4*

INGREDIENTS
1 French loaf
4 redfish, black bream or porgy, each
    weighing about 275 g/10 oz
15 ml/1 tbsp vegetable oil
1 mango
1 cm/½ in fresh root ginger
1 fresh red chilli, seeded and finely
    chopped
30 ml/2 tbsp lime juice
30 ml/2 tbsp chopped fresh coriander
175 g/6 oz young spinach
150 g/5 oz pak choi
175 g/6 oz cherry tomatoes, halved

*spinach*

*coriander*

*root ginger*

*porgy*

*cherry tomatoes*

*mango*

**1** Pre-heat the oven to 180°C/350°F/Gas mark 4. Cut the French loaf into 20 cm/8 in lengths. Slice lengthways, then cut into thick fingers. Place the bread on a baking-sheet and dry in the oven for 15 minutes. Pre-heat the grill (broiler) or light the barbecue and allow the embers to settle. Slash the fish deeply on both sides and moisten with oil. Grill (broil) or barbecue for 6 minutes, turning once.

**2** Place one half of the mango flesh in a food processor. Peel the ginger, grate finely, then add with the chilli, lime juice and coriander. Process until smooth. Adjust to a pouring consistency with 30–45 ml/2–3 tbsp water.

**3** Wash the salad leaves and spin dry, then distribute them between 4 plates. Place the fish over the leaves. Spoon on the mango dressing and finish with slices of mango and tomato halves. Serve with fingers of crispy French bread.

## COOK'S TIP
Other varieties of fish suitable for this salad include salmon, monkfish, tuna, sea bass and halibut.

# Egg and Lemon Mayonnaise

This recipe draws on the contrasting flavours of egg and lemon, with the chopped parsley providing a fresh finish – perfect for potato salad. Serve with an assortment of cold meats or fish for a simple, tasty meal.

*Serves 4*

INGREDIENTS
900 g/2 lb new potatoes, scrubbed or scraped
salt and pepper
1 medium onion, finely chopped
1 egg, hard-boiled
300 ml/10 fl oz/1¼ cups mayonnaise
1 clove garlic, crushed
finely grated zest and juice of 1 lemon
60 ml/4 tbsp chopped fresh parsley

## COOK'S TIP

At certain times of the year potatoes are inclined to fall apart when boiled. This usually coincides with the end of a particular season when potatoes become starchy. Early-season varieties are therefore best for making salads.

egg

garlic

onion

lemon

new potatoes

**1** Bring the potatoes to the boil in a saucepan of salted water. Simmer for 20 minutes. Drain and allow to cool. Cut the potatoes into large dice, season well and combine with the onion.

**2** Shell the hard-boiled egg and grate into a mixing bowl, then add the mayonnaise. Combine the garlic and lemon zest and juice in a small bowl and stir into the mayonnaise.

**3** Fold in the chopped parsley, mix thoroughly into the potatoes and serve.

# Crème Anglais

Here is the classic English custard, light, creamy and delicious – far superior to packet versions. Serve hot or cold.

*Serves 4*

INGREDIENTS
1 vanilla pod
450ml/³/₄ pint/1⁷/₈ cups milk
40 g/1¹/₂ oz/3 tbsp caster sugar
4 egg yolks

*milk*

*vanilla pod*

*eggs*

*caster sugar*

**1** Split the vanilla pod and place in a saucepan with the milk. Bring slowly to the boil. Remove from the heat, then cover and infuse for 10 minutes before removing the pod.

**2** Beat together the sugar and egg yolk until thick, light and creamy.

**3** Slowly pour the warm milk on to the egg mixture, stirring constantly.

**4** Transfer to the top of a double boiler or place the bowl over a saucepan of hot water. Stir constantly over a low heat for 10 minutes or until the mixture coats the back of the spoon. Remove from the heat immediately as curdling will occur if the custard is allowed to simmer.

**5** Strain the custard into a jug if serving hot or, if serving cold, strain into a bowl and cover the surface with buttered paper or clear film.

## VARIATION

Infuse a few strips of thinly pared lemon or orange rind with the milk, instead of the vanilla pod.

## COOK'S TIP

To help prevent curdling, blend 5 ml/1 tsp of cornflour with the egg yolks and sugar.

# Chocolate Fudge Sauce

A real treat if you're not counting calories. Fabulous with scoops of vanilla ice-cream.

*Serves 6*

INGREDIENTS
150 ml/¼ pint/⅔ cup double
  cream
50 g/2 oz/4 tbsp butter
50 g/2 oz/¼ cup vanilla sugar
175 g/6 oz plain chocolate
30 ml/2 tbsp brandy

## VARIATIONS

White Chocolate and Orange
Sauce:
40 g/1½ oz/3 tbsp caster sugar,
  to replace vanilla sugar
175 g/6 oz white chocolate, to
  replace plain chocolate
30 ml/2 tbsp orange liqueur, to
  replace brandy
finely grated rind of 1 orange

Coffee Chocolate Fudge:
50 g/2 oz/¼ cup light brown
  sugar, to replace vanilla sugar
30 ml/2 tbsp coffee liqueur or
  dark rum, to replace brandy
15 ml/1 tbsp coffee essence

*vanilla sugar*

*brandy*

*plain chocolate*

*butter*

*double cream*

**1** Heat the cream with the butter and sugar in the top of a double boiler or in a bowl over a saucepan of hot water. Stir until smooth, then cool

**2** Break the chocolate into the cream. Stir until it is melted and thoroughly combined.

**3** Stir in the brandy a little at a time, then cool to room temperature.

**4** For the White Chocolate and Orange Sauce, heat the cream and butter with the sugar and orange rind in the top of a double boiler, until dissolved. Then, follow the recipe to the end, but using white chocolate and orange liqueur instead.

**5** For the Coffee Chocolate Fudge, follow the recipe, using light brown sugar and coffee liqueur or rum. Stir in the coffee essence at the end.

**6** Serve the sauce over cream-filled profiteroles, and serve any that is leftover separately.

# Ginger and Honey Syrup

Particularly good for winter puddings, this sauce can be served hot or cold.

*Serves 4*

INGREDIENTS
1 lemon
4 green cardamom pods
1 cinnamon stick
150 ml/¼ pint/⅔ cup runny
  honey
30 ml/2 tbsp ginger syrup, from
  the jar
3 pieces stem ginger

*green cardamom pods*

*cinnamon stick*

*lemon*

*honey*

*stem ginger*

**1** Thinly pare 2 strips of rind from the lemon with a potato peeler.

**2** Lightly crush the cardamom pods with the back of a heavy-bladed knife.

**3** Place the lemon rind, cardamom, cinnamon stick, honey and ginger syrup in a heavy-based saucepan with 60 ml/4 tbsp water. Bring to the boil and simmer for 2 minutes.

**4** Chop the ginger and stir into the sauce with the juice of half the lemon. Pour over a winter fruit salad of poached dried fruits and sliced oranges. Chill to serve.

## VARIATION
To serve hot with steamed puddings, strain at the end of step 3 before stirring in the stem ginger and lemon.

# Sabayon

Serve this frothy sauce hot over steamed puddings or chill as shown and serve just as it is with light dessert biscuits or whatever you prefer. Never let it stand, as it will collapse.

## *Serves 4-6*

INGREDIENTS
1 egg
2 egg yolks
75 g/3 oz/²/₃ cup caster sugar
150 ml/¹/₄ pint/²/₃ cup sweet
   white wine
finely grated rind and juice of
   1 lemon

*lemon*

*sweet white wine*

*egg yolks*

*eggs*

*caster sugar*

**1** Whisk the egg, yolks and sugar until they are pale and thick.

**2** Stand the bowl over a saucepan of hot – not boiling – water. Add the wine and lemon juice, a little at a time, whisking vigorously.

**3** Continue whisking until the mixture is thick enough to leave a trail. Whisk in the lemon rind. If serving hot serve immediately over pudding or fruit salad.

**4** To serve cold, place over a bowl of iced water and whisk until chilled. Pour into small glasses and serve at once.

## COOK'S TIP
A generous pinch of arrowroot whisked together with the egg yolks and sugar will prevent the sauce collapsing too quickly.

# Butterscotch Sauce

A deliciously sweet sauce which will be loved by adults and children alike! Serve with ice-cream or with pancakes or waffles.

## Serves 4-6

INGREDIENTS
75 g/3 oz/$\frac{1}{3}$ cup butter
175 g/6 oz/$\frac{3}{4}$ cup soft dark
  brown sugar
175 ml/6 fl oz/$\frac{3}{4}$ cup
  evaporated milk
50 g/2 oz/$\frac{1}{2}$ cup hazelnuts

*soft dark brown sugar*

*evaporated milk*

*hazelnuts*

*butter*

**1** Melt the butter and sugar in a heavy-based pan, bring to the boil and boil for 2 minutes. Cool for 5 minutes.

**2** Heat the evaporated milk to just below boiling point, then gradually stir into the sugar mixture. Cook over a low heat for 2 minutes, stirring frequently.

**3** Spread the hazelnuts on a baking sheet and toast under a hot grill.

**4** Tip on to a clean tea towel and rub briskly to remove the skins.

**5** Chop the nuts roughly and stir into the sauce. Serve hot, poured over scoops of vanilla ice-cream and warm waffles or pancakes.

## VARIATION

Substitute any nut for the hazelnuts, pecans, for example, add a luxurious flavour. You could also add plump, juicy raisins and a dash of rum instead of the nuts.

# Redcurrant and Raspberry Coulis

A dessert sauce for the height of summer to serve with light meringues and fruit sorbets. Make it particularly pretty with a decoration of fresh flowers and leaves.

*Serves 6*

INGREDIENTS

225 g/8 oz redcurrants
450 g/1 lb raspberries
50 g/2 oz/¼ cup icing sugar
15 ml/1 tbsp cornflour
juice of 1 orange
30 ml/2 tbsp double cream

*orange*

*icing sugar*

*double cream*

*cornflour*

*redcurrants and raspberries*

**1** Strip the redcurrants from their stalks using a fork. Place in a food processor or blender with the raspberries and sugar, and purée until it is smooth.

**2** Press the mixture through a fine sieve into a bowl and discard the seeds and pulp.

**3** Blend the cornflour with the orange juice then stir into the fruit purée. Transfer to a saucepan and bring to the boil, stirring continuously, and cook for 1–2 minutes until smooth and thick. Leave until cold.

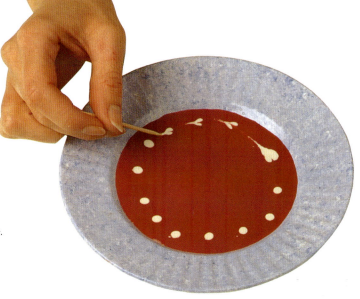

**4** Spoon the sauce over each plate. Drip the cream from a teaspoon to make small dots evenly around the edge. Draw a cocktail stick through the dots to form heart shapes. Scoop or spoon sorbet into the middle and decorate with flowers.

# Lemon and Lime Sauce

A tangy, refreshing sauce to end a heavy meal, it goes well with pancakes or fruit tarts.

*Serves 4*

INGREDIENTS
1 lemon
2 limes
50 g/2 oz/¼ cup caster sugar
25 ml/1½ tbsp arrowroot
300 ml/½ pint/1¼ cups water
lemon balm or mint, to garnish

*limes*

*arrowroot*

*caster sugar*

*lemon*

**1** Using a citrus zester, peel the rinds thinly from the lemon and limes. Squeeze the juice from the fruit.

**2** Place the rind in a pan, cover with water and bring to the boil. Drain through a sieve and reserve the rind.

## VARIATION

This sauce can also be made with orange and lemon rind if you prefer, and makes an ideal accompaniment for a rich orange or mandarin cheesecake.

**3** In a small bowl, mix a little sugar with the arrowroot. Blend in enough water to give a smooth paste. Heat the remaining water, pour in the arrowroot, and stir continuously until the sauce boils and thickens.

**4** Stir in the remaining sugar, citrus juice and reserved rind, and serve hot with freshly made pancakes. Decorate with lemon balm or mint.

# Brandy Butter

Traditionally served with Christmas pudding and mince pies, but a good spoonful on a hot baked apple is equally delicious.

*Serves 6*

INGREDIENTS
100 g/4 oz/$\frac{1}{2}$ cup butter
100 g/4 oz/$\frac{1}{2}$ cup icing, caster or
   soft light brown sugar
45 ml/3 tbsp brandy

*butter*

*soft light
brown sugar*

**1**   Cream the butter until very pale and soft.

**2**   Beat in the sugar gradually.

**3**   Add the brandy, a few drops at a time, beating continuously. Add enough for a good flavour but take care it does not curdle.

**4**   Pile into a small serving dish and allow to harden. Alternatively, spread on to aluminium foil and chill until firm. Cut into shapes with small fancy cutters.

**brandy**

## VARIATION
**Cumberland Rum Butter**
Use soft light brown sugar and rum instead of brandy. Beat in the grated rind of 1 orange and a good pinch of mixed spice with the sugar.

# Pineapple and Passion Fruit Salsa

Pile this fruity dessert salsa into brandy snap baskets or meringue nests.

## Serves 6

INGREDIENTS
1 small fresh pineapple
2 passion fruit
150 ml/¼ pint/⅔ cup Greek-style
  yogurt
30 ml/2 tbsp light muscovado sugar

*pineapple*

*passion fruit*

*Greek-style yogurt*

*muscovado sugar*

**1** Cut off the top and bottom of the pineapple so that it will stand firmly on a chopping board. Using a large sharp knife, slice off the peel.

**2** Use a small sharp knife to carefully cut out the eyes.

**3** Slice the pineapple and use a small pastry cutter to stamp out the tough core. Finely chop the flesh.

**4** Halve the passion fruit and scoop out the seeds and pulp into a bowl.

**5** Stir in the chopped pineapple and yogurt. Cover and chill.

**6** Stir in the sugar just before serving the salsa.

## VARIATION
Lightly whipped double cream can be used instead of Greek-style yogurt.

# Mixed Melon Salsa

A combination of two very different melons gives this salsa an exciting flavour and texture.

*Serves 10*

INGREDIENTS
1 small orange-fleshed melon, such
 as Charentais
1 large wedge watermelon
2 oranges

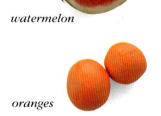
*Charentais
melon*

*watermelon*

*oranges*

**1** Quarter the orange-fleshed melon and remove the seeds.

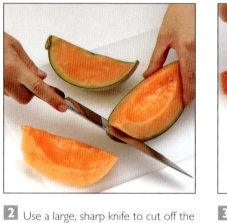

**2** Use a large, sharp knife to cut off the skin. Dice the flesh.

**3** Pick out the seeds from the watermelon then remove the skin. Dice the flesh into small chunks.

**4** Use a zester to pare long strips of rind from both oranges.

**5** Halve the oranges and squeeze out all their juice.

**6** Mix both types of the melon and the orange rind and juice. Chill for about 30 minutes and serve.

## VARIATION
Other melons can be used for this salsa. For example, try cantaloupe, Galia or Ogen.

# Papaya and Coconut Dip

Sweet and smooth papaya teams up well with rich coconut cream to make a luscious sweet dip.

### Serves 6

INGREDIENTS
2 ripe papayas
200 ml/7 fl oz/scant 1 cup
   crème fraîche
1 piece stem ginger
fresh coconut, to decorate

*papayas*

*crème fraîche*

*stem ginger*

*fresh coconut*

**1** Halve each papaya lengthways, then scoop out and discard the seeds. Cut a few slices and reserve for decoration.

**2** Scoop out the flesh and process it until smooth in a blender or a food processor.

**3** Stir in the crème fraîche and process until well blended. Finely chop the stem ginger and stir it into the mixture, then chill until ready to serve.

**4** Pierce a hole in the "eye" of the coconut and drain off the liquid, then break open the coconut. Hold it securely in one hand and hit it sharply with a hammer.

**5** Remove the shell from a piece of coconut, then snap the nut into pieces no wider than 2 cm/¾ in.

**6** Use a swivel-bladed vegetable peeler to shave off 2 cm/¾ in lengths of coconut. Scatter these over the dip with the reserved papaya before serving.

## COOK'S TIP
If fresh coconut is not available, buy coconut strands and lightly toast in a hot oven until golden.

# Raspberry Salad with Mango Custard Sauce

This remarkable salad unites the sharp quality of fresh raspberries with a special custard made from rich fragrant mangoes.

*Serves 4*

INGREDIENTS
1 large mango
3 egg yolks
30 ml/2 tbsp caster (superfine) sugar
10 ml/2 tsp cornflour (cornstarch)
200 ml/7 fl oz/scant 1 cup milk
8 sprigs fresh mint

RASPBERRY SAUCE
500 g/1 lb 2 oz raspberries
45 ml/3 tbsp caster sugar

*eggs*

*mint*

*mango*

*raspberries*

**1** To prepare the mango, remove the top and bottom with a serrated knife. Cut away the outer skin, then remove the flesh by cutting either side of the flat central stone. Save one half of the fruit for decoration and roughly chop the remainder.

**2** For the custard, combine the egg yolks, sugar, cornflour and 30 ml/2 tbsp of the milk smoothly in a bowl.

**3** Rinse a small saucepan out with cold water to prevent the milk from catching. Bring the rest of the milk to the boil in the pan, pour it over the ingredients in the bowl and stir evenly.

**4** Sieve the mixture back into the saucepan, stir to a simmer and allow the mixture to thicken.

**5** Pour the custard into a food processor, add the chopped mango and blend until smooth. Allow to cool.

## COOK'S TIP

Mangoes are ripe when they yield to gentle pressure in the hand. Some varieties show a red-gold or yellow flush when they are ready to eat.

**6** To make the raspberry sauce, place 350 g/12 oz of the raspberries in a stain-resistant saucepan. Add the sugar, soften over a gentle heat and simmer for 5 minutes. Rub the fruit through a fine nylon sieve to remove the seeds. Allow to cool.

**7** Spoon the raspberry sauce and mango custard into 2 pools on 4 plates. Slice the reserved mango and fan out or arrange in a pattern over the raspberry sauce. Scatter fresh raspberries over the mango custard. Decorate with 2 sprigs of mint and serve.

# Strawberries with Raspberry and Passion Fruit Sauce

Fragrant strawberries release their finest flavour when moistened with a sauce of fresh raspberries and scented passion fruit.

*Serves 4*

INGREDIENTS
350 g/12 oz raspberries, fresh or
   frozen
45 ml/3 tbsp caster (superfine) sugar
1 passion fruit
700 g/1½ lb small strawberries
8 plain finger biscuits (butter
   cookies), to serve

*biscuits (cookies)*

*passion fruit*

*raspberries*

*strawberries*

**1** Place the raspberries and sugar into a stain-resistant saucepan and soften over a gentle heat to release the juices. Simmer for 5 minutes. Allow to cool.

**2** Halve the passion fruit and scoop out the seeds and juice.

**3** Turn the raspberries into a food processor or blender, add the passion fruit and blend smoothly.

188

## COOK'S TIP

Berry fruits offer their best flavour when served at room temperature.

**4** Pass the fruit sauce through a fine nylon sieve to remove the seeds.

**5** Fold the strawberries into the sauce, then spoon into 4 stemmed glasses. Serve with plain finger biscuits (butter cookies).

# INDEX